INSIDE VIEW

OF

SLAVERY:

OR A

TOUR AMONG THE PLANTERS.

BY C. G. PARSONS, M. D.,
WITH AN INTRODUCTORY NOTE BY
MRS. H. B. STOWE.

FOURTH THOUSAND.

BOSTON:
PUBLISHED BY JOHN P. JEWETT AND COMPANY.
CLEVELAND, OHIO:
JEWETT, PROCTOR AND WORTHINGTON.
1855.

B. THURSTON
Electrotyper, and Steam Printer,
Portland, Maine.

PREFATORY NOTE. — The following work is little more than a record of facts seen and learned during an extensive tour in the Southern States in 1852 and 1853, from a journal made at the time. This tour was made, and the notes had been used by the author as the basis of a series of lectures delivered in several of the New England States, before any other "view" of slavery had been published. Neither its origin nor its preparation has been induced, therefore, by any publication that has preceded it.

The manuscript copy, as originally prepared for the press, contained the entire names of individuals and places. At the suggestion of the publisher many of these names have been suppressed, or the initials only inserted. But as this has been done solely from a regard for the feelings of the individuals referred to, — many of whom are the author's personal friends, — any one desiring to obtain the names, with the view of testing the truth of any statements contained in the volume, can do so by applying to him, or to the publisher. C. G. P.

Windham, Aug. 1, 1855.

INSIDE VIEW OF SLAVERY.

"When Freedom, on her natal day,
Within her war-rocked cradle lay,
An iron race around her stood,
Baptized her infant brow in blood,
And, through the storm which round her swept,
Their constant ward and watching kept.

* * * * * * * * *

"Our fathers to their graves have gone
Their strife is past, — their triumph won;
But sterner trials wait the race
Which rises in their honored place —
A moral warfare with the crime
And folly of an evil time.

"So let it be. In God's own might
We gird us for the coming fight,
And, strong in Him whose cause is ours,
In conflict with unholy powers,
We grasp the weapons He has given, —
The Light, and Truth, and Love of Heaven!"

WHITTIER.

CONTENTS.

CHAPTER. PAGE

INTRODUCTION — *By Mrs. H. B. Stowe,* - 11

I. — PRELIMINARY REMARKS, - - - - - - - - 13

II. — ARRIVAL AT SAVANNAH, - - - - - - - 20

III. — ARE THE SLAVES CONTENTED? - - - - 29

IV. — CHRISTMAS IN SAVANNAH, - - - - - - 40

V. — ILLUSIONS OF SLAVERY, - - - - - - - - 53

VI. — WHY THE NORTH PROSPERS, - - - - 62

VII. — RESOURCES OF THE SOUTH, - - - - - - 67

VIII. — SOUTHERN AGRICULTURE, - - - - - 78

IX. — YANKEE AND SLAVEHOLDER COMPARED, - 96

X. — PRIVATE AND PUBLIC BUILDINGS, - - - 106

XI. — THE PARTING SCENE, - - - - - - - 118

XII. — SLAVEHOLDERS AS BUSINESS MEN, - - 125

XIII. — SOUTHERN SPORTS, - - - - - - - 135

XIV. — TREATMENT OF SLAVES, - - - - - - 150

XV.—Footprints of Slavery, ... 163
XVI.—No Sympathy for Slaves, ... 173
XVII.—Southern Jurisprudence, ... 186
XVIII.—Slavery Hardens the Heart, . . 203
XIX.—Slavery and Education, ... 232
XX.—Slavery and the Sabbath, ... 254
XXI.—Slavery and Christianity, ... 269
XXII.—Wayside Notes, ... 286
XXIII.—The Giant Slave, ... 300
XXIV.—The Ethiopian Socrates, ... 311

INTRODUCTION.

WE have in this book the simple, straightforward narrative of an impartial witness, whose relationships and business brought him into intimate connections with all the phases of Southern society.

It is truly, as its title indicates, an *inside view of slavery*,—a view which could only be taken by one brought into intimate association with tho society described.

It appears to be candid and fair in its spirit—to extenuate nothing, nor set down ought in malice,—and the facts carry their own authentication with them.

We recommend to all unprejudiced, or even prejudiced persons, to *read* it. If they once begin, they will not be likely to leave before the book is finished. And having read it, we hope they will ask themselves the question — are these things so? — and if they are, — have *I* any duties to perform respecting them? Every man, woman, and child in America has a personal interest in the question—what is slavery? — and every person is morally bound to form a correct opinion with regard to it.

This book is earnestly commended, therefore, to the attention of all who wish an intelligent answer to that question.

H. B. Stowe.

Andover, August 8th, 1855.

INSIDE VIEW OF SLAVERY.

I.

A TOUR AMONG THE PLANTERS.

"Oh! come to the South, where my servants shall all
Depart at thy bidding, and come at thy call, —
Where the shade of the palm tree is over my home,
And the lemon and orange are white in their bloom!"

One of the most interesting features of the age in which we live, is the spirit of reform that everywhere pervades it. It is confined to no nation or country. The whole civilized world is alive with it. Before its searching scrutiny, no abuse is allowed to pass unnoticed. It finds its way into the prisons and cloisters of Europe, to deliver their inmates, or ameliorate their condition. It attacks despotism, alike in church and state. It strikes at systems hoary with age and crime, and exposes their enormities; — while it brings the habits and practices of men, — though sanctioned by fashion and custom, — to the test of its searching scrutiny. Like Ithuriel's spear, it touches everything, however disguised, that tends to degrade, or injure, or debase mankind, and reveals it to the world, in all its native ugliness and deformity.

This spirit, as now developed with special prominence in this country, relates to the two great evils of the land,—slavery, and intemperance. I do not mean to say that it is limited to these. It has no limit, within the range of human welfare. But as these evils are now engrossing a large share of public attention, so the voice of reform is calling loudly for some way of deliverance. The question of remedy is more properly within the sphere of political discussion;—but the evils themselves, as they deeply affect moral, social, and physical life, enter into almost every field of literary effort.

The observations which have resulted in the preparation of this volume were made more minutely, as well as more extensively, in Georgia than in any other State. The early settlement of that State was begun under more favorable auspices than attended the birth of any other,—not excepting even Massachusetts. The founders of the colony of Georgia seem to have had some premonitions of the evils that were afterwards to afflict our country,—and they sought to avert them. Under their first charter, therefore, *the introduction of slavery, and the importation of spirituous liquors were both expressly prohibited.* How different would have been the condition of that State, and, perhaps, of the whole nation, if those provisions had been maintained to this day!

But the adjacent colony of South Carolina was thickly populated with slaves, and the evil example was contagious. Like the ancient Hebrews when they desired a king, — wishing to be like their neighbors, they at length became so. As the population increased, and the inhabitants became closely connected in business, the anti-slavery clause in their code began to be violated with impunity, and in 1749 it was abrogated.

The same struggle and defeat on the temperance question had already been seen. As early as 1736 a cargo of liquors, brought into Savannah by the Carolina traders, was seized by the civil authorities, and publicly destroyed, — and the traders were imprisoned. Perhaps nothing in the early colonial histories approaches nearer to the "Maine Law" than this. But it was too far in advance of the age, to stand. Adverse influences from the neighboring colonies, — especially from South Carolina, — together with the power of appetite and interest at home, finally gained the victory, — and the prohibition was removed.

There are few Northern men who have not relatives, or intimate friends, in the South. State sovereignty and citizenship, local attachments, the sacred associations of home, all yield to the centrifugal forces of active life, and families are scattered until, perhaps, each member resides in a different State. But the strong ties of early affection, though lacerated, are not destroyed. The companions of childhood are remembered, and if we are not able to revisit them among

> "The smiling hills, the spacious, fertile vales,
> Where oft we wandered, plucking vernal flowers,
> And reveled in the odor-breathing gales,

we long for them to visit us where another home has

been hallowed by new associations. And hence, though there are repulsions in religion and politics, and sectional controversies have arisen, the warm greeting and kind invitation are still sent and returned. And, thanks to a good Providence, whatever have been the recriminations of politicians, and whatever blemishes there may be upon the character of our people, either North or South, this spirit of generous hospitality and warm-hearted social intercourse is not yet dead!

From the commencement of the anti-slavery movement in this country, I have been deeply interested in its progress; and though I have never believed it necessary, in order to understand this subject, that one should visit the slave States, still I had long wished to do so. I felt certain that there must be, among the effects of the slave system, facts that would arrest the attention and awaken the sympathy of Northern men more than could be done by discussing its abstract principles. I therefore determined to know, from actual observation, *the workings and results of this system.*

In the autumn of 1852, I made my arrangements for a tour in the Southern States. I had a number of relatives in Georgia whom I desired to visit; and as some of them were slaveholders, and all of them so situated that a more intimate acquaintance with their southern homes would bring me into close contact with slavery, I designed to avail myself of every opportunity which the occasion might afford for a thorough investigation. The fact that I had influential friends connected with the system, gave me, probably, a nearer access to its secret operations than had ever been enjoyed by any one not supposed to be in favor of it. The *time* of my visit was also opportune, being after the compromise measures had been adopted in Congress. The pulpit and the press had proclaimed that all "agitation had ceased," and that the "anti-slavery cause was dead." In the South this was, to some extent, believed to be true; and the *espionage* of slaveholders over the movements of Northern men was less than had been known before for many years.

During my sojourn in the South, I traveled through Florida, Alabama, Tennessee, Virginia, and the Carolinas. Thus I learned that the *agricultural* system of all the slave States is generally the same. But my inquiries into the condition and the business habits of the people, the institutions of learning and religion, and the whole *modus operandi* of the slave system, in its effects upon masters, non-slaveholders, and slaves, were made more particularly in the State of Georgia. And, perhaps, no single State exhibits a fairer view of the whole system. Though not in so mild a form as in Virginia and Maryland, still darker and more cruel aspects of it may be seen in the Carolinas, and the South Western States.

In order to obtain a correct knowledge of the manners and customs of the people, and their modes of doing business, I engaged, at different times, in various occupations. In no other way can a *stranger* become acquainted with men and things. For some time I traveled in the interior, as agent for a commission house in the city of Savannah, purchasing cotton, corn, hides, &c. At another time I was employed by a lumber company that was building mills in the country, to superintend the operation, and take charge of the manufacturing business. Here were slaveholders and slaves laboring together, living in log cabins, eating from the same dish, and sleeping on the same floor, or on the ground, at night. One of the owners was a Presbyterian clergyman, and a slaveholder, but the smartest man to work we had in the "crowd." The "master builder" was also a minister, of the Baptist denomination. He was a native Georgian, but a thorough going abolitionist. The subject of slavery was frequently and fully discussed among us, and its injurious effects on industrial pursuits were admitted by all.

No one can understand much of slavery by looking at the features which it presents in the northern slave States. The influence of free labor, and Northern institutions, here modifies the system, and either banishes or conceals many barbarous practices which are common farther south. The master, even if unconscious of it, feels the influence of public sentiment, and often seeks to palliate the great wrong by kind treatment.

Neither can any one see and know what slavery is *by visiting only the cities and large villages* in the southern slave States. Here, as in the States farther north, the slaveholder is surrounded by influences that change the external features of the system, and tend to check its excesses. Those men who are prominent in the learned professions, and most successful in business, are many, if not most of them, from the North. If we inquire of the most enterprising, wealthy merchants in the cities, not only on the coast, but in the interior of the slave States, where they originated, they will point us to their remote country homes in New England, where they first saw the light, where their early years of life were employed in vigorous exercise on the rough farm in summer, and in the common school in winter. These men learned the value of schools and churches before they left their good old puritan homes, and they have struggled manfully to maintain these institutions, in spite of the downward tendencies, and the untoward influences of the slave system. And they have also *felt* that *laboring men* need wholesome, nutritious food to stimulate the muscle, and quiet rest at night, on a comfortable bed, to restore tone to the nerves. Such men care for the condition of their servants. The legitimate effects of slavery are not fully developed in their families, though the slaves probably experience great sufferings in the best condition, which the stranger cannot perceive, nor even the master know.

But to understand what slavery is, we must go into the planting districts, and see the "*live Crackers*," as the inhabitants of those districts are familiarly called. Here we behold the native slaveholder alone with his slaves, having no Northern men about him to influence his conduct, to check the full indulgence of his appetites, or restrain his passions. Here, and here only, can we see slavery as it is. No where else are its legitimate results and real influences so fully disclosed.

II.

A TOUR AMONG THE PLANTERS.

"By storied hill and hallowed grot,
By mossy wood and marshy glen,
Whence rang of old the rifle shot,
And hurrying shout of Marion's men,
The groan of breaking hearts is there —
The falling lash, the fetters' clank!
Slaves — *slaves* are breathing in that air,
Which old DeKalb and Sumpter drank!

WHITTIER.

THE Southern Colonies did not distinguish themselves in the Revolutionary War. Savannah and Charleston successively surrendered to the British arms, and at last, Georgia and both the Carolinas were abandoned to the British power. The Southern army was nearly destroyed, and the remnant withdrawn from the field. And yet, these colonies were the scenes of some of the most brilliant exploits and heroic adventures that are recorded in the history of that memorable struggle. The death of Pulaski, and DeKalb, the daring bravery of Gen. Sumpter as he contested the ground, inch by inch, with a superior force, before which he was compelled at last to retire, the struggles and triumphs of Marion, Wayne, and Morgan, after Gen. Greene had taken the command of the Southern division of the army, form a chapter of events not inferior in interest to any other. It was from this field that Kennedy gathered the materials for his fine historical romance "Horse-shoe Robinson." And whatever may be said of the devotion which the South exhibited to the American cause during the Revolutionary War, it must be admitted that since that time she has held the names of the heroes who fought and bled upon her soil in grateful remembrance. Her counties, cities, and towns are named in honor of them, and the places consecrated by their struggles are pointed out to strangers as shrines of patriotic devotion. In a public square in the city of Savannah, a monument has been erected to the memory of Gen. Greene,—and another to commemorate the fame of Count Pulaski, who fell during the gallant but unsuccessful attempt to retake the city, by Gen. Lincoln, in 1779.

I arrived in Savannah on the 22d of November, 1852. This city is located upon the river of the same name, 18 miles from its mouth. The site is an elevated sandy plain, about forty feet above the level of the river, the bank of which was originally called "Yamacraw Bluff;" a name, like that of the river itself, of Indian origin. The earliest settlement in the State was at this place. The city was laid out by Gen. Oglethorpe, in 1733, and has always been the largest commercial depot on the Atlantic coast, south of Charleston. The British took possession of it in 1778, and held it until 1783. A large portion of it was destroyed by fire in 1820, but so far from checking its prosperity, this disaster resulted in its permanent improvement. It was unhealthy in summer, until the rice growers were induced, by a contribution of $70,000 from the citizens, to abandon the practice of flowing the rice fields in the vicinity. The dry cultivation of rice is substituted, but to less profit. The river is navigable as far as Augusta, 230 miles from its mouth. This, with several railroads by which Savannah is connected with the interior, makes it the center of a large amount of inland trade. About 350,000 bales of cotton are annually received and shipped here, and in 1852, there were exported from this city 40,000 casks of rice, and 25,000,000 feet of lumber. In 1853 the population was 23,000, of whom about 10,000 were colored.

The city stands upon a sandy plain, or table land. It is regularly laid out with wide, unpaved streets. At every alternate corner, there is reserved a public square, planted with ornamental trees. The most of these are the Pride of India tree, which are very far from being beautiful in foliage, or fragrant in blossom. Since my return to the North, I have learned that a large part of them have been destroyed by a violent wind,— and if some other kind of tree shall be substituted for this, in a few years no one will regret the loss.

In the rear of the city is a public park, containing forty acres, mostly covered with the original pine trees, standing so far apart as not to prevent the growth of grass, and enclosed by a high, costly, iron fence.

The monument to Count Pulaski, before mentioned, though wanting in proportion and symmetry, is an honor to the city, and an ornament to the beautiful square in front of the large hotel by the same name.

No one of the fourteen churches would be called elegant, except the Independent Presbyterian, which is truly magnificent. It cost $120,000. It is built of light marble, and has wide aisles with marble floors. Retreating sky-blue niches between the windows, for monuments, add beauty to the interior; and the whole edifice, both within and without, for symmetry and beauty is probably not surpassed in the country.

Savannah exhibits unmistakable signs of enterprise, refinement, and wealth. Many of the dwelling houses are spacious and elegant, the stores are large and well filled. In the heart of the city every thing imparts to the view of the stranger an idea of comfort; but in the suburbs, the low, dingy, dirty, squalid, cheerless negro huts, remind the Northern visitor of the fearful price paid by one class to support another.

The principal business is based on the great staple, cotton. During my first visit to the place, nine trains came down the Central Railroad daily, with from twenty to thirty cars in each train, loaded mountain high with this article. The depots and plank yards, covering several acres, were groaning constantly under the immense burden, while long trains of horse teams were laboring for their relief, by drawing it over a plank road a mile or more in length, to the commission houses. Samples of the various descriptions of cotton are displayed in the ante-rooms of the stores, into which purchasers are introduced, and contracts are made so privately and quickly that it is difficult for a Yankee to find out whether any business is done at all. But the clerks are standing, silent, at their desks, dashing their pens for their lives. Bills, orders, checks, drafts, are exchanged, bales of cotton are passing into vessels from the wharves as fast and still as ripe blossoms from the trees in the spring-time, when shaken with a strong east wind.

I spent more time in Savannah than in any other Southern city. From this place I made my excursions for business, or observation, or pleasure, and having accomplished the object in view, returned here again, to form new plans, or complete my notes of slavery in city life. In short, I made this a sort of *point d'appui*, if I may use a military phrase, around which the operations of my Southern tour were carried on. And it was fortunate for my purpose that I took this course. For though the true features of slavery may generally be seen in the country without much trouble, it is not so in the city, as has already been noticed. It is only by a protracted residence, and a careful examination, that the real condition of the slaves can here be understood. And even then, there are many who have had no special reasons for investigating this subject, who know but little about it. I have known Northern men who have lived in Southern cities many years, without ascertaining whether slaves, belonging to families in which they reside, have wholesome food, *or comfortable beds.*

A few weeks before I left Savannah for the interior, I boarded at the Marshall House. A friend of mine who had boarded at the same house for several years, and who had become an advocate of slavery, not having witnessed much of the privations and sufferings of slaves, frequently inquired of me if the slaves in that city did not appear to be in a better condition than the colored population of the North. And I was constrained to admit that, *so far as I had been able to judge from what I had seen,* the slaves were very well cared for. But before I left that house, some facts came to my knowledge, in relation to the treatment of slaves at the public boarding houses, which astonished some of the Yankees who had been there for years. And the disclosures show that business relations afford the best opportunities for obtaining facts.

Mr. L., of Maine, contracted with the proprietor of the Marshall House for a lease of those premises for several years. The keys were put into his hands on the third morning of January, 1853. When Mr. L. opened the bar-room door, he found three of the male servants sleeping on narrow boards placed on chairs, the floor being sanded, without a pillow or a blanket. He opened the boot room, and there found two of the "boot blacks," in a room too short for them to lie down at full length, with nothing but boots for pillows. In the kitchen, there were five female cooks sleeping on the solid brick hearth. This fact was not disclosed to the Northern boarders until this gentleman had taken charge of the house. My friend, though he had boarded there two years, had not known until that morning, that Mr. Johnson's slaves had no beds. Mr. L. inquired of Mr. J., if there were no beds furnished, and sleeping apartments appropriated to the slaves?

"No," replied Mr. J.; "niggers never sleep on beds in the public houses in this State."

I mentioned to a gentleman of my acquaintance who was boarding at the Pulaski House, that we had made the discovery at the Marshall House, that the slaves had no beds to rest upon; to which he replied,

"Mr. Johnson is a brute, not to furnish his negroes with beds, for they have to work very hard here in winter."

"Do they have beds at your house?" I asked.

"Of course they do," was the reply.

"Are you sure? Because Mr. Johnson says they never have beds at the taverns."

The next day, my friend told me that he had asked the proprietor at the Pulaski House what kind of beds were furnished for his servants.

"Beds!" exclaimed Capt. W., "don't you know that niggers never sleep on beds? Put any one of my niggers on the best bed there is in my house, and he wont lie there half an hour. Niggers prefer sleeping on the floor."

This was the largest hotel in the State, and its patrons were among the wealthiest and most refined. There were some fifty slaves, or more, owned or employed about the establishment, as it is necessary to have many more servants in a first class hotel in the South than in the North. And yet, this gentleman had boarded there some years, and having no special interest in making the inquiry, he had not learned that the slaves who waited upon him by day and by night, were never provided with even such beds as Northern farmers furnish their horses.

One of the first strange sights to a Northern man on visiting the cotton-growing States, is the enormous quantity of this article that he sees wherever he goes. In the streets, in the storehouses, on the wharves, it is constantly before him. He will no longer wonder that Gen. Jackson made a breastwork of it in defending New Orleans. At or near the railroad depot in Savannah, there are, sometimes, literally, acres of cotton bales. Standing in view of it, and remembering that this city is but *one* of the depots for this trade, he can comprehend, to some extent, the remarkable influence which this great American staple exerts, not only upon industrial pursuits, but upon the business, and even upon the politics of the country.

My first impression was that, as nearly all the cotton raised in Georgia was shipped from this port, I should find Savannah frequented from day to day by cotton-growers from the interior. But I was mistaken. Occasionally a specimen of the "Crackers" may be seen at a hotel, but no one can form any correct opinion of the manners, customs, or the intelligence of the people in the back counties by anything which he will see on the seaboard. Their habits are entirely different from those of business men in the North. I found, before leaving the South, that there was very little intercourse between the inhabitants of the planting districts and the cities on the coast.

I traveled over the Central Railroad six times, from Savannah to Macon, a flourishing inland city, containing some 7000 inhabitants. This road is the great thoroughfare from the interior to the seaboard. Only one passenger car was ever attached to the train. At one time, on a fair day, there were only twelve passengers on board. The highest number at any time was only thirty-five.

The "Crackers" send their negroes and mule teams with the cotton to their agents at the railroad depots. These agents forward it to the commission merchants in the ports. The merchants sell it to shippers, and the planters draw on them, at the banks, for their pay. So that there is no necessity for them to go to market themselves. And any one who visits the country remote from the seaboard, will find many slaveholders, who are in easy circumstances, who have never seen a vessel, or a printing press.

As a general thing, also, the "Crackers" are very ignorant. And I may as well state a fact here, which I did not learn until some time after I first visited Savannah. There are few Northern men who are not capable of ascertaining the quantity, and computing the value, of whatever they send to market. I dare say the instance was never known, of a Northern farmer sending his pressed hay to be sold, without having it weighed and marked, and knowing himself the amount. But the cotton-grower is frequently incapable of weighing and marking his cotton, and is, therefore, obliged to send it unmarked, and trust entirely to the honesty of the merchant who acts as his agent.

III.

ARE THE SLAVES CONTENTED?

"The slave happy! You may place him where you please; — you may dry up, to your utmost, the fountain of his feelings, the springs of his thought; — you may close upon his mind every avenue to knowledge, and cloud it over with artificial night; — you may yoke him to your labor, as the ox which liveth only to work; — you may put him under any process which, without destroying his value as a slave, will debase and crush him as a rational being; — you may do this, and the idea that he was born to be free will survive it all. It is allied to his hopes of immortality; it is the eternal part of his nature, which oppression cannot reach. It is a torch lit up in his soul by the hand of the Deity, that can never be extinguished by the hand of man."

MC. DOWELL, OF VIRGINIA.

NORTHERN men and women who visit their relations in the South, usually find them in the cities and villages, where they see the slaves enjoying the comforts of a poor bed, and other privileges, which slaves in the country seldom, if ever, enjoy. They are liable, therefore, to form too favorable opinions of the condition and treatment of the slaves; and they often honestly arrive at the conclusion that they are in a better condition than the poor colored population of the North.

Sometimes one is allowed to inquire of the slaves themselves how they fare. The answer, almost invariably, is, that they fare well — have kind masters — are contented and happy — do not desire their freedom if it can only be obtained by leaving the family of their master, and their good home, to which they are ardently attached; — and the inquirer decides that the Northern abolitionists have greatly exaggerated their sufferings. He does not know that the slave has been educated to deceive in these matters; and he believes that he is contented and happy, simply because he says so.

At a hotel where I was boarding, in the city of Savannah, there was a christian slave named "John." His wife had been torn away from him, and carried into the back country a distance of twenty five miles. John's affection was so strong that he had several times "run away" to see her, though he was always whipped severely on his return. At last his master told him that he must give up the old wife, and take a new one. Accordingly, he "bought a wife for John," and commanded the slave to regard and treat her as his wife. John refused to obey, and was whipped, again and again, but he did not yield. A Northern gentleman, who was not acquainted with these facts, had frequently asserted that the slaves were happy, and I suggested that inquiries be made of "*honest John*" touching his domestic enjoyments. The bell was rung, and John came in.

"Now, John," said my friend, "I want you to tell me if you would like to be free."

"O no, master," replied John, quickly. "I don't want to be free, no how."

"Then you have a kind master, have you, John?"

"Yes, I have a kind master, and I don't want to be sold away."

"Then you prefer to stay with your present master

John, rather than to be made free, or go to any other place to live, you say?"

"I reckon I rather remain here," answered John, "because I don't know what worse hands I may fall into."

"There, now what do you say," said the gentleman, turning to me, "about the discontent of the slaves?"

"I think John has deceived you, sir," I replied.

"How so?"

"Has he satisfied you that he is contented and happy?"

"Most certainly. I have no doubt he is so."

"In this you are entirely mistaken, sir, and John sees it, but he dare not undeceive you. I secured his confidence a few days ago, and he told me the story of his wrongs, and afflictions, and sufferings.

"And now, John," said I, "will you state the facts connected with your treatment on account of your wife, that my friend here, who is also your friend, may know the truth in this matter? Speak freely; you shall not be betrayed."

John then threw off the mask, and stated the simple facts. The affecting story would melt any heart except that of a slaveholder. The Northern merchant acknowledged that he he was never before so artfully deceived. And these false representations, which the slaves are compelled to make for their own security, have kept Northern men in ignorance of their true condition.

The following incidents will show how liable we are to be deceived in the cities of the South, by having the best aspects of slavery presented to us; and also what duplicity is practised upon us by the slaveholders for this purpose.

Among the boarders at the hotel where I stopped were Mr. N. and his excellent christian lady. They were members of the Presbyterian Church. Mr. N. was a cotton broker, a native of that State, and owned a plantation and slaves in the country. He was a warm friend of the temperance cause, in which I had expressed a deep interest publicly in that city. While making a call at his private room, where I found him and his lady alone, after conversing upon the subject of temperance awhile, Mr. N. asked me if I was an abolitionist. He said that he had been so informed by one of my Northern friends.

I replied that he had been correctly informed.

"Are you a Garrisonite?" he asked.

I answered, that I was not.

"You are a political abolitionist, then, I presume?"

"Yes, sir, you are right; I am a political abolitionist, and I profess to be a *moral and religious* abolitionist, also."

"Well, now, let me say to you," said Mr. N., "that I have been North, during the summer, for several years, visiting the cities, and Springs, and Falls, where I have read your anti-slavery papers, — not only those of the Garrison school, but Bailey's, and Leavitt's, and others, — and let me tell you, sir, that, if you have taken your views of slavery from those papers, you have formed erroneous opinions of the institution. You will find the slaves in a much better condition than that which is described in those fanatical papers. Most of the writers in those papers have never traveled in the South, to see for themselves how well the slaves fare. Now if you examine closely, you will see that the slaves are well cared for, in every respect. You will not find the cruelty and the suffering you have expected to see."

"I have no doubt, sir," he added, positively, "that you will have your views of slavery essentially modified, and return to the North with your opinions in relation to this whole subject entirely changed."

This was said with so much apparent sincerity, and I had reposed so much confidence in the integrity of Mr. N., that he actually inspired me with the hope, at least, that I should find the slaves in a better state than I had anticipated.

This interview was had previous to my traveling in the country; but subsequent disclosures of the sufferings and privations of the slaves at that public house, led me to suspect that Mr. N. intended to deceive me. And especially after I had traveled among the "Crackers," and had been permitted to lift the veil and take an *inside view* of the system, in all its forms, I knew that he intended to misrepresent the case, and make a false impression upon my mind.

On my return to that city, just before I left the South, I called on Mr. N. again, and found him and his excellent lady alone, as before. I was greeted very cordially. During this conversation, I remarked to Mr. N. that I had taken the liberty to call to ask him a simple, straightforward question, to which I wanted him to give me an honest, explicit, christian answer.

"Well, what is it, sir, you wish to know?" inquired Mr. N., with evident surprise, and a little embarrassment.

"It is this, sir" I replied. "Will you inform me

why you stated to me, when I first came to this city, that the slaves were well treated, that the anti-slavery papers of the North had belied the slaveholders, and that I should find good reasons, by a careful examination of the system, for changing my abolition views?"

"To tell you the plain truth," said Mr. N., with a blush and a laugh mingled in the expression, "I did not know then that you were intending to go out into the country!"

"I told Mr. N., after you left us at that time, sir," said Mrs. N., quickly, "that he had deceived you; and the only apology he made for it was, that slavery would never be abolished, that you could do nothing to make the condition of the slave better, and that you might as well be sent home to the North with your heart and mind put to rest on that matter, as to have you trouble yourself any farther about it."

Mr. N. did not deny that his good lady had given me the true explanation of his equivocal conduct and language.

By arts like these has many a Northern man been sent home to peddle South-side notions in Yankeedom. Slavery is a shrewd, practiced, and cunning dissembler. Like Milton's Comus,

"it hurls
Its dazzling spells into the spungy air,
Of power to cheat the eye with blear illusion,
And give it false presentments; * *
And, under fair pretence of friendly ends,
And well placed words of glozing courtesy,
Baited with reasons not unplausible,
Winds itself into easy-hearted men,
And hugs them in its snares."

A wealthy planter, from the interior of the State, was introduced to me, in the city of S., before I traveled in the interior, for the purpose, as I afterwards ascertained, of deceiving me with reference to the treatment of slaves in his neighborhood.

I had been previously assured, by a friend, that this gentleman enjoyed a reputation entirely above suspicion for honor and integrity, and I could therefore place the fullest confidence in his statements. His manner of conversation aided to confirm a favorable impression of his reliability.

During our interview, several topics relating to slavery were discussed, and, among others, the feeding of slaves.

I inquired how the slaves were fed in his part of the State.

He replied, "that formerly they were not so well fed as at that time. The planters," he said, "have found it more profitable to treat the slaves kindly and feed them well, as they would perform more labor, and take a deeper interest in the master's welfare. Therefore they have adopted a system of high feeding."

"Do you give your slaves as much meat as they want, Colonel?" I inquired.

"*Meat!*" said he, with a laugh; "I feed my hands on the best, most costly, and nutritious articles which the market affords, such as eggs, poultry, fresh meats, butter, &c., and just as much as they are disposed to eat."

"Indeed! And do your neighbors feed in the same manner?"

"Yes, sir, most of my neighbors feed in the same

way; and I can assure you it is altogether the best way. Provisions are generally cheap in this State, and hands that are well fed have better health, and do more work; and we find it to be the most profitable way, after all, to feed well."

I was really surprised at this; and yet it was all true. But still it left a false impression on my mind, which I should probably have brought home with me, had I not afterwards visited the place where Colonel H. resides, and learned "the other side of the story." The "*sunny side*" gave me only *half* the truth. When the other half from the "shady side" was brought to the light, and the two halves were joined together, the whole truth gave the fullest evidence that the slaves in that neighborhood suffered more by severe treatment from exacting, rigorous masters, than in any other part of the State.

Let us walk in and see the slaves of the "reliable" Col. H. Let us go into the huts, and out upon the plantations, and see with our eyes a well fed, "kindly treated" family of slaves.

"Whose field is that on the other side of the creek?" said a Northern gentleman, who was traveling with me, to a neighbor of Col. H.

"That is a plantation of negroes the Colonel hires this year, I believe," replied the "Cracker."

"Will there be any harm in our going over there to see the boys work?"

"I reckon you had better go and see the Colonel *first*," answered his neighbor, "for he is mighty particular about allowing strangers around among his people."

"Will you be so kind, sir, as to direct us to the Colonel's house?" said I.

"There comes his old boy, 'Monday,' now. He will show you up there, sir."

"Thank you, sir."

"Ho, Monday! This way! We want you to go and show us the way to your master's house."

"Well, I can't go now, master. I must go down to the store first, and get a gun for young master William. He is up at the school house you see there by the great tree, and he will tell you where the folks live."

We passed on to the log school house, where, much to our joy, we found a Yankee shool teacher — an old acquaintance.

The school was left to take care of itself awhile. I made inquiries respecting Col. H. and his slaves, repeated the statements he made to me, and expressed my great surprise to learn that slaves were fed in the manner stated by him.

"Ah! there is *another side* to that story!" exclaimed the teacher. "That gentleman *bet five thousund dollars* last year that he could raise more cotton with his hands than a neighbor could with the same number."

The truth now flashed upon me. I could see a motive now for feeding high. The slaves were to be driven hard. The man who raised the largest amount of cotton would gain the five thousand dollars, in addition to the product of the field.

"Costly and nutritious food was supplied to those

slaves," said the teacher of that school, "and the cotton-planter's whip was as freely *applied* to them."

The Colonel's plantation was close by that school room.

"The driver," said he, "went behind the gang of slaves, constantly cracking his whip, from morning till night. The boy or girl that fell in the rear received the lash, just like the poor, feeble lamb that falls behind in the drove. And I was informed," he added, in a tone expressing great grief and sympathy, "that *eighteen slaves* belonging to that man perished in the fields and huts last summer, from being over driven. But Col. H. raised more cotton than the neighbor with whom he laid the wager."

"How much cotton did he raise?" I asked.

"About fifty thousand dollars' worth, I have heard," said the teacher.

"With how many hands?" I inquired.

"Four hundred, I believe."

The amount of cotton raised probably exceeded, by some fifteen or twenty thousand dollars in value, the usual crop obtained under the ordinary mode of feeding and driving. In both respects the case was an exception, proving nothing but the fact that, whether well or ill fed, kindly or cruelly treated, the slave is completely in the power of his master, with no source of protection, no power of resistance, no hope of redress.

No one can travel in the South without seeing that the system of slavery has no "abuses," — that what he has been accustomed to regard as such are only the legitimate fruits, or rather the constituent elements of the system itself. All the cruelties and the tortures, — so far as required to enforce submission, — the sundering of families, the degradation, and the wholesale concubinage, are inseparable from the system. If the system is right, it is right that any "privilege and appurtenance" required to perpetuate it should be included in the deed. If it is right to hold a man in bondage, it is right to take his wife from him, sell his children, keep him ignorant of the word of God, chain him, whip him, take his life, if he refuses to yield. Deny any of these, and you leave no security for a permanent possession of the man.

The feelings of our common nature rise in rebellion against such a system. In the words of one of England's most gifted orators, "Be the appeal made to the understanding or the heart, the sentence is the same that rejects it. There is a law above all the enactments of human codes, — the same throughout the world, — the same in all times, — and by that law, unchangeable and eternal, while men despise fraud, and loath rapine, and abhor blood, they will reject, with indignation, the wild and guilty phantasy, that *man can hold property in man!*"

IV.

CHRISTMAS IN SAVANNAH.

"They were red-hot with drinking;
So full of valor that they smote the air
For breathing in their faces; beat the ground
For kissing of their feet." SHAKESPEARE.

Mr. J. was landlord of the "Marshall House," in the city of S. He had a beautiful negro boy named John; sometimes called "Little John," to distinguish him from an older slave boy of the same name, belonging to Mr. J.

I have said little John was a *beautiful boy,* and so said all the boarders, even the lady boarders from the North. From this fact, some of my Northern readers will infer that Johnny was a white boy. They entertain so deep a prejudice against the African that they cannot associate an idea of the beautiful with a black complexion. But Johnny was a "real black" boy. His form was elegant, his head as "pretty shaped" as any white boy's head — a good forehead, and very thin lips, for a negro. But his courteous manners, mild disposition, good conduct, and kind heart, made him more beautiful.

Besides, little Johnny had excellent common sense, and talked with such propriety, and his voice was so musical, and soft, and persuasive, and captivating, that everybody was charmed with everything he said, and delighted with everything he did.

Mr. L., a Yankee boarder, had been negotiating with Mr. J., for a lease of the House; and so nearly was the bargain completed, the report ran through the house that the proprietor's keys were to be put into the hands of Mr. L. the next morning.

All the slaves expect Christmas presents from friends and boarders, and all "to whom they yield themselves servants to obey," during Christmas week.

Johnny had received many presents both from Mr. L. and his amiable lady, who had often spoken to him with words of more kindness and sympathy than slaves are wont to hear addressed to them by the whites. Encouraged by these expressions of interest in his welfare, which he had fondly treasured in his warm, confiding heart, he ran up to Mr. L. on the last day of Christmas, —for Christmas lasts till January—and said, "Mr. L., I want you to give me a dollar!"

"A dollar! Johnny?" replied Mr. L., "that is a great Christmas present. What are you going to do with a dollar?"

Emboldened by the recollection of the former kind words and deeds of Mr. L., and inspired by his own trusting nature, he answered with deep emotion:

"I am going to keep it, Mr. L."

"What are you going to keep it for, Johnny?" asked Mr. L., smiling.

"I don't like to tell you, Mr. L.," was the almost suppressed reply.

"Don't like to tell me, Johnny? Why not?" asked Mr. L. again.

"I am afraid you will tell Master J.," whispered Johnny, as there were other gentlemen present.

"If I give you a dollar, Johnny," added Mr. L., "your master will get it away from you."

"No he wont!" said Johnny earnestly. "I tell you I am going to keep it, Mr. L."

"Well now, Johnny," said Mr. L., "if you will tell me the object for which you want to keep it, and can satisfy me that it will ever do you any good, I will certainly give you a dollar."

"Now, then, I will tell you, Mr. L.," said Johnny, feeling re-assured, "and I know you wont tell Master Johnson. I am going to keep all the money I can get, so when I get enough, I can buy my FREEDOM!!"

The last word, "freedom," was spoken aloud, and exhibited so much of the spirit and genius of Liberty — such a deep, innate, impassioned desire to be free, that Mr. L. could withhold the dollar no longer. And that was not the only dollar added to little Johnny's consecrated treasure, by which he fondly, but vainly, hoped at some future day to purchase the restoration of his "inalienable rights."

It was rumored that Mr. J. had great *liabilities* at the return of Christmas, but not so great as John's. Both were liable to be intoxicated, but the poor boy had the additional liability to pay for it in a whipping. And so it proved this time, to his sorrow.

His young mistress, Miss C., had a new, rich silk dress.

Unfortunate little Johnny, staggering as he went by Miss C., spilled some burning fluid on the large, elegant cape of her splendid dress, which entirely ruined the beauty of that costly, dazzling drapery.

Mr. J. was informed by his *amiable* lady the next morning, that John had spoiled their daughter's new dress by his carelessness. The master, greatly enraged at this communication from the mistress, vociferously uttered in tones of bitter complaint towards the boy, started to run down the narrow walk to the kitchen, and met John coming up the walk to the dining room. He caught the boy by the throat, exclaiming, "Now you scoundrel, I'll pay you for spoiling C.'s dress!" And he threw him on the floor, jumped on him with his hard heeled winter boots, and stamped on his breast and face, mangling him in a most shocking manner! After he stepped off, the slave did not move! He seemed not to breathe, and Mr. J. ran into Mr. L.'s room, near by, who was expected to take possession of the house in a few days, and exclaimed, "I wish you would come out, Mr. L.! I believe I have killed John!"

"Killed John! How?" said Mr. L.

"I only chastised him a little for getting drunk, and spoiling C.'s dress."

Mr. L. ran into the walk. John had begun to breathe again; other signs of returning life soon followed; servants were called, and the helpless boy was carried off into some dark apartment, where he was not seen again by the boarders for three weeks. When he returned to his services as waiter at the table, more than half his face was still covered with the bruises. The broken-hearted, broken-spirited Johnny was never so blithsome and sprightly, and genial-hearted, and happy, after his "joyous, jolly Christmas" was succeeded by that terrible stamping, which well-nigh terminated his life; and all the fond dreams he had cherished of his future freedom had vanished, for his money was NOT TO BE FOUND!

A mulatto boy named "Joe," about this time ran away into the woods. The steward, a hot-blooded, iron-hearted Spaniard, who was constantly whipping some of the servants, had threatened to whip Joe, for some misdemeanor on one of the Christmas days; and to avoid the whipping, which he dreaded as much as death, he ran off. He was a young boy, not over twelve years of age, and had no idea of running away in search of freedom, or another home; but he ran out into the woods, near the city, having no thought in his plan but to escape the whipping,—not even deciding in his own mind how long he should remain in the woods, or whether he should ever return to his master's house. He staid in the woods five days, until he was almost famished with hunger. He then decided to return to the house in the evening, and gain access to the room of his mistress secretly, and appeal to her for protection from the brutal steward. He succeeded in gaining the ear, but not the sympathy of his mistress. She immediately reported the return of the runaway to the steward, who settled with the poor, emaciated, suffering boy, for his Christmas sins,

> "With stripes, that mercy weeps
> To see inflicted on a beast."

Mr. J. and his wife were "Crackers." They owned a plantation in the country, where they had always lived until within a year or two, — and there is no sympathy for "niggers" in the country. Conversation turned, one evening, upon the subject of catching runaways, and a lady from Maine remarked that she had "*heard* of their setting dogs on the tracks of the slaves when they ran away, and that the dogs often bit them, but she never believed it."

"Well, you had better believe it, Mrs. L.," said a daughter of Mr. J., "for father used to keep twenty-five hounds, to catch niggers with. I have seen the runaway niggers brought in, with large junks bitten out of their arms and legs, big enough to fry."

This was spoken with apparently as little pity for the slave, as she would feel for the dead hog, when speaking of cutting up legs of bacon.

Joe's running away was not the only calamity of the kind that visited Mr. J.'s family during the holidays. One of his sons ran away with another fellow, like himself, already a drunkard. They were thoughtful enough to take bottles of whiskey with them, but took little money in their sacks. Johnson's son had suffered so much at home, that he declared to his comrade he would shoot his father if he overtook them and attempted to take them back. The father, after pursuing them several days, found them down in *Liberty* county.

When the profligate son saw his father drawing nigh, on horseback, he drew his pistol to shoot him; but the father took out a bottle of whiskey from his portmanteau, and brandished that in sight of the thirsty, whiskey-loving son, — whose empty bottles admonished him of his folly in leaving a father's house, where there was whiskey enough and to spare, — and the heart of the truant relented. With humble confession for his deep ingratitude, the father received him with great joy and mirth.

Many a time, after most of the boarders had retired at night, reports of pistols were heard in adjoining rooms. Sudden calls for the doctor to attend cases of delirium tremens, in the house, were numerous during Christmas. The Georgia physicians say that the enervating Southern climate induces this disease, as the Northern rigorous climate does consumption. But if the climate is the only exciting cause of delirium tremens, in Georgia, it is more to be avoided through fear of premature death, than the tendencies to consumption in Maine; for more adult, free, male inhabitants of that State, die annually of delirium tremens, than die in Maine of consumption.

A Christian lady of Maine, who had read and heard accounts of the destructive influence of the habits of dissipation upon young men in the South, became alarmed for the safety of her son, who was employed as a clerk, in Macon, Georgia, and she sent her request for him to return home.

While at Macon, Mr. L. formed an intimate acquaintance with twelve young men — clerks in that city — seven of whom were from the North. At this request of his mother,

"whose pious care
Shielded his infant innocence with prayer,"

Mr. L. came back to the North. I was with him, ten years afterwards, when he visited Macon again, and inquired for one after another of his old comrades.

"Where is George?"

"Dead!" replied an old friend.

"Where is Ben?"

"Dead!"

"Where is Frank?"

"Dead!"

"What was the matter?"

"Delirium tremens!"

And, to be brief, ten of those young men had gone into drunkards' graves by delirium tremens,— one was an idiot,— and the last insane. There was not a man among the twelve with whom he could shake hands and be recognized as a friend, when only ten years previous, they were all enterprising young men, from eighteen to twenty-two years of age. Mr. L. confessed that he formed a very favorable opinion of slavery the first year he spent in Macon, but he was now brought to a position where he could see one of its most terrible results, and he instantly turned his thoughts gratefully towards his mother, whose prayers and fidelity had saved him. "Had not my mother been faithful," he said to me, "doubtless I should have shared the same sad fate that has cut down my unfortunate friends!"

Mr. L. is now an active business man in New England, whose credibility no one will question.

But I am inclined to the belief that the Maine Law, well executed in the slave States, would subdue the predisposing causes to delirium tremens, — while the habits of the South, if introduced into New England, would not diminish the tables of mortality by consumption.

While I was sitting on the stone sidewalk in front of the Marshall House, conversing with Mr. Johnson, one of the Christmas evenings, three, heavy, cut-glass tumblers were thrown from a window of a room in the third story, and came down upon the sidewalk near our seats, with a startling crash. Anon, plates, and knives and forks, and small articles of furniture were thrown out further into the street. One large platter was thrown out into the middle of the street, by one of the Kentuckians who occupied that chamber. The platter fell in the "horse-bed," directly before a horse and buggy, passing at that instant. The horse stepped into the platter, breaking it in many pieces, and, taking fright at the noise, he ran away with the gentlemen in the carriage.

The young Kentuckians, sons of slaveholders, came down to S., with a drove of horses and mules which their fathers gave them for a Christmas present, and, having sold them, they were spending the effects of the sale to suit their taste. Mr. J. uttered a round oath against the rowdies, and then started to go to the chamber to ascertain what they were doing. It was very convenient for me to be passing up to my room at the time Mr. J. rapped at the door of the Kentuckians' room, on the same floor.

"Who 's there?" halloed one of the b'hoys.

"Johnson," replied the host.

"What do you want?"

"I want to come in here."

"You sha'nt come in, sir."

"Yes I will come in," replied Mr. J.

"If you come in here, we will shoot you."

"Very well, boys," said Mr. Johnson, gruffly, and left the room to its fate, at the mercy of a Christmas revel.

The next morning, I happened to be at the office when the Kentuckians settled their bill. One of them asked,

"Well, Mr. J., what is the bill?"

"I have looked at the bill of furniture I put into that room," said Mr. J., "and I find it amounted to just seventy dollars. I suppose you have smashed it all up."

"Very like," replied the Kentuckian; and he added, "I am sure that what is left is of no account, sir!"

The seventy dollars in addition to the regular fare, were paid, and the party left.

The following day, in conversation with Mrs. C., wife of a hardware merchant of that city, I was expressing my astonishment that those young men would spend so large a sum of money for such a foolish gratification. That excellent lady, who was a native of Savannah, remarked that that was a small amount, compared with what is frequently paid for such "busts" by young men at the South, whose fathers are wealthy; and then she related the following facts:

There was a young man who came to this city, and received several thousand dollars at a bank, for cotton his father had sent to this market. He was a fast young man, and he concluded to have a frolic before he left the city for his home in the back part of the State. So he bought a little box gig, and took it to the smith and ordered the axletree cut off at each end, to bring the wheels close up to the body of the carriage, making it so narrow that it would ply along the narrow sidewalks in that city. He then hired the fleetest horse and had him harnessed into the gig on Sabbath morning; and after the church bells had called the people out upon the walks, the reckless youth sprang into his gig, and drove around the city on the sidewalks, driving the women and children into the middle of the streets of sand, screaming for their lives.

The police were called, and they pursued the disturber of the peace; but they were unable to catch him. Coming around in front of the Pulaski House — the largest hotel in the city — the wide bar-room doors, which open directly into the street, being open, he drove his team into that bar-room, discharged a pistol towards the barkeeper, the bullet entering the wall just above his head, whirled his horse before he could be seized by the bridle, turned about and dashed into the street again, and drove until the horse became weary, so that the police were enabled to take him.

They carried him to the Pulaski House. Capt. W. looked at the gentleman, saw that he was "well dressed," and inferring that he had a long purse, told him that he must pay *five hundred dollars.*

"Cheap enough!" replied the rowdy, complacently. "I have had a good frolic!"

The money was paid over, and thus the affair was

settled, to the "satisfaction" of all the church-going folks in that Christian city.

Few young men who go South from the free States, to engage in business, retain the steady habits of their Northern education. A friend of the writer, in New York, had a son employed as clerk in a cotton store at S., with a salary of a thousand dollars. But this sum was insufficient to meet the expenses of that fashionable clerk, and he drew on his father quite often to pay up arrears for board. The father addressed me a note, requesting that I would, if possible, ascertain the cause of this draft upon him, and desired me to learn the habits of his son, and inform him. On the father's account, I took occasion to notice the conduct of his son while at the bar-room, one evening soon after.

It is customary at the South among young men of that class, to drink large quantities of wine or other liquors; but when reciprocating a treat with comrades, they take a much less quantity at a time than is taken at the North. Sometimes, in the South, the "convivial" glass passes several times in an hour. When the Southron intends to have a "soak," he takes the bottle to his bed-side, goes to bed, and lies there till he gets drunk and becomes sober, and then he gets up.

My young friend H. W. came in from his store that night, stepped to the bar, and called for spirits. He drank a small quantity, turned around, saw an old acquaintance, called for more. In a few minutes after, some other comrades came in. He drank with them and they with him, by turns, and so in the course of one short hour, the *young gentleman* took eight social drinks; but not more than a table spoon-full at each time. He drew his purse, paid a dollar to the bar-keeper for the treat; then ordered a bottle of wine to his room, and paid a half eagle for that. Six dollars a day for liquor! TWO THOUSAND ONE HUNDRED AND NINETY DOLLARS A YEAR!

V.

ILLUSIONS OF THE SYSTEM.

"What man so wise, what earthly wit so ware,
As to descry the crafty, cunning train,
By which deceit doth mask in visor fair,
And cast her colors, dyed deep in grain,
To seem like truth, whose shape she well can feign,
And fitting gestures to her purpose frame,
The guileless man with guile to entertain!"

SPENSER'S FAIRY QUEEN.

No man can visit the South for the first time without having his views of slavery, whatever they may be, to some extent modified. If he is credulous, disposed to believe that everything is really what it seems to be, that the surface of society mirrors that which lies beneath, as well as that which is above it, — if he credits all that is told him, and looks at slavery through the slaveholder's glasses, he will return home with a south-side view, and his acquaintances in the South will laugh at his credulity. But if he takes nothing on trust, examines everything for himself, engages in business, and gains the confidence of the slaves, so that he can feel their hearts beat and throb against the great wrong, and look at the system with *their* eyes instead of their *master's*, "remembering those in bonds *as bound with them,*" he will wonder at his own coldness hitherto. And from his new position he will understand some of the ways in which men have been deceived, or have deceived themselves on this subject.

There is one source of delusion, on this subject, of which few seem to be aware. It lies in the power of a *name* to chill our sympathies, and pervert our moral convictions. The term *slave* has a definite meaning. It signifies, not a person, but a thing, a chattel; and an immense advantage has been secured to the pro-slavery side of the argument from Scripture, by virtually changing our own translation from *servant* to *slave.* Even anti-slavery men write and talk about Hebrew *slaves* instead of servants, and thus yield half the force of their arguments by the use of the term.

More than this, the Southern bondman is likely to lose more than half his worth, in our estimation, when we think and speak of him as a *slave,* instead of a man, oppressed and in bondage. It is very difficult for one to resist this influence of a *name* on his own mind. When we have called a man a slave, we shall probably find, if we analyze our thoughts, that we have degraded him below the level of manhood, in our practical estimation. and the wrongs he suffers seem to lose a great measure of the enormity we should attach to them if inflicted on a man. Our sympathies are moved when the *slave* is starved, scourged, tortured; but it is not so much because his *manhood* is degraded as because the *animal* is suffering.

Such being the influence upon ourselves, it is not

strange that those who have been trained in the midst of the corrupting system, and taught to regard the slave as a mere chattel, without personal rights, should exercise little sympathy for his wrongs.

I intend no disrespect to clergymen, when I say that no class of men have so little knowledge of men and things as some of the most learned theologians, who from boyhood have been shut up to schools and books. They have enjoyed little opportunity to learn the workings of human nature among the mass of mankind, — they are therefore poorly qualified to investigate the ordinary business of life, or to look into other men's matters. Their training may have been favorable to purity of mind and manners; it has removed them from many of the corrupting influences of society; but for this very reason they are unqualified to examine the workings of a system whose influence pervades every interest, every employment, and every thought of the community.

They have visited the South, and brought back their reports of its effects on the varied interests and institutions of the country. They naturally make their inquiries of the same class of men, who themselves know little of slavery except its fairer aspects, or, if they do know, are careful to hide its most revolting features; and they return as ignorant of the workings and influence of slavery as they went.

And I also found it to be true, though with some exceptions, that clergymen in Southern cities are not well informed as to the condition of the slave. The means of accurate information on this subject are not enjoyed in the South. It is not freely discussed there. The welfare of the slave is seldom a topic of conversation. His condition is below the consideration of the higher classes.

A clergyman, eminent for piety, talent, and learning, assured me that he had resided in one of the most populous cities of the South several years without having the opportunity afforded him to look into the practical operation of the system.

"And probably," said he, "I should have remained in ignorance of the destructive effects of the system to this day, had not a Northern minister of my own denomination come down to make me a visit. He prevailed on me to make a tour with him through the country. We went out through the Carolinas, Georgia, and Alabama, over to the Mississippi River, and down to New Orleans. Then we came back in another direction, through the planting districts, and we saw that slavery ruined everything that it touched. We were astonished at every step to witness its destructive influence on everything valuable. I was most surprised at my own ignorance of the condition of the inhabitants of the planting districts. They are miserable beyond description."

"I am willing," he added, "to make all due allowance for the disabilities of the master, struggling against adverse influences; but I must confess to you, sir, that I am an abolitionist. If slavery is not abolished soon, it will ruin the whole country. The tendency of the system is to make men idle and vicious, and consequently ignorant and degraded."

"Why really, sir," said I, "you admit all the evils we have ever charged against the system. If I should talk about slavery after I go home as you do now, some of your Northern ministerial brethren would say it was fanatical, and an exaggeration."

"Exaggeration!" exclaimed the reverend gentleman, "impossible! You can not exaggerate when speaking of the evils of slavery! The pit has not been uncovered yet. If it ever is, and the North are permitted to look into it, they will pronounce it '*the bottomless pit!*'"

"Good men here in the South," he added, "know very little of the shocking cruelties perpetrated on the defenceless slaves. And, indeed, but little is known in the cities of the wretchedness and poverty of most of the *whites* in the country. No good man can *know* what the system is doing to us all, and not *detest* it; much less, apologize for it, or connect himself with it."

And yet this minister was not known by his society to be an abolitionist. He thought that it would do no good to the slaves for him to speak out his real feelings on this subject, and that by doing so he would lose all his influence, and be driven from his field of labor. Hence he only uttered his opinions where they would not be used against him. There are many like him in the South. It is not my province to judge them. They weep *in secret* over the sins of the people. Would to Heaven that they had the courage to lift up their voices, "cry aloud and spare not," though compelled in consequence to shake off the dust of their feet against them!

It is also true, as strange as it may appear, that there

are many slaveholders who know but very little about the condition of the slaves. Statesmen, lawyers, and even merchants, who own plantations, spend very little time upon them, and know scarcely anything which occurs there, except what is reported to them by their overseers.

I had a conversation on the subject of slavery with a Southern clergyman, who was well acquainted with John C. Calhoun. During the interview, I made frequent allusions to the ultra pro-slavery doctrines of this great statesman, and expressed my want of confidence in the integrity of a man who gave all the influence of his great name, and employed all his talent, and learning, and logic, to build up such an institution. But his clerical friend, who had admitted to me his own hatred of the system, apologized for Mr. Calhoun's apparent inconsistency.

"Mr. Calhoun," said he, "knew nothing about slavery."

"Is it possible, sir?" said I. "I have always inferred, from the manner he wrote about it, that he must be perfectly acquainted with the operations of the system. Will you do me the favor to explain your statement, —that he knew nothing about it?"

"I will, sir. Mr. Calhoun, it is well known, was a kind, benevolent slaveholder. He gave orders to have his slaves well fed and clothed, but he did not condescend to visit his kitchens and slave huts to see whether his directions were obeyed. He always kept more servants, in every department of his family, than were necessary to perform the labor required, so that his house-servants were not overworked. No slave of Mr. C.'s was afraid at any time to ask his master, in person, for a dollar to supply any want, nor had any fears of being turned away empty, if he could convince him that he really needed the favor he asked. That constant inclination to supply every known want of his servants, and the positive instructions invariably given to the "managers" of his slaves, constituted the whole of his personal care for them. Farther than that, the happiness of his slaves was a thing not included with the bounds of his thoughts."

"But," I inquired, "could he not see the instances of cruelty and suffering among other slaves, whom he saw in his daily walks?"

"No, sir, he did not stop for that, nor think of it. The class of slaveholders to which Mr. C. belonged, do not come down to enter the walks in life where the sufferings of the slaves can be seen. If they hear one writhing under the lash, they lend no ear to his cry. They presume that the punishment is merited. It is the conventional law of society, that no white man shall listen to the story of the slave's wrongs from his own lips."

"What aristocrats the slaveholders are!" I exclaimed.

"You do not hit Mr. Calhoun with that remark," said his friend, "for he was no aristocrat, I assure you. When he employed a *white* man in his service, — a carpenter, for instance, about his house, — that carpenter sat down with Mr. C. to eat at his table, and he conversed with him as an equal. In this respect he set a worthy example to your Northern aristocrats. He often spoke of the aristocracy of Northern capitalists, as manifested in their treatment of their free white laborers. Mr. C. ever regarded a white man as his equal. The badge of a slave only, disentitled a man to his companionship."

"When Mr. Calhoun visited any of his friends," the gentleman continued, "especially in the country, he would of course send a note some time previous, informing them at what time they might expect to entertain himself and family. Then when he arrived at the house of his friend, he found everything put in preparation to receive him. The servants were all dressed finely, looking neat and cheerful. He gave them all little presents, as is customary in such families, which made the slaves appear very happy and joyous. It was in such circumstances that Mr. Calhoun saw the slaves of the South.

"Then when he went North, and noticed the degraded condition of the free colored man in your cities, — often having no one to care for him, nobody offering him profitable employment, none aiding him to obtain knowledge, or assisting to elevate him in society, Mr. C. came to the conclusion that slavery was the best condition of the African race. I have no doubt he honestly believed that the white man was born with a scepter in his hand, and that the black man was created to be his servant."

Such was the apology which this gentleman offered for the great Southern statesman. How much weight it should be allowed to have in extenuation of Mr. Calhoun's inveterate devotion to the slave system, it is not for me to say. But I have no doubt of the general truth before stated, that many slaveholders are ignorant on this subject. And in judging of any of them it ought not to be forgotten that persons living in the midst of slavery gradually become familiar with its attendant evils, and by imperceptible degrees they come to view calmly exhibitions of cruelty and suffering from which they would once have shrunk with horror.

VI.

WHY THE NORTH PROSPERS.

"Labour is life! — 'T is the still water faileth;
Idleness ever despaireth, bewaileth;
Keep the watch wound, or the dark rust assaileth;
Flowers droop and die in the stillness of noon.
Labour is glory! — the flying cloud lightens;
Only the waving wing changes and brightens;
Idle hearts only the dark future frightens;
Play the sweet keys would'st thou keep them in tune!"

FRANCES S. OSGOOD.

It is the superior physical education of the North, — the practical knowledge, and the advantages derived from the various kinds of labor to which her whole people are devoted — that best qualifies them for the ordinary business of life. The young man must *work*, as well as *think*, that the muscles may mature while the mind is being developed, or he will not succeed in any profession. "No man," says a learned physician, "ever enjoyed perfect health who was brought up in *idleness*." The superior intellectual character of the people of New England is to be attributed mainly to their early habits of industry, which give them athletic physical systems for vigorous minds to work in.

"As an humble farmer's son, upon the granite hills of New England," says Horace Greely, "I became early inured to constant toil, and learned not merely to confront labor, but to respect it, — to recognize its stern afflictions as one of the greatest blessings which Heaven sends. It is a necessary and vital safeguard against falling into the depths of depravity and misery. Through it alone has our race, or any part of it, ever risen in the scale of moral being. Moral degradation has always first come upon those who have felt least heavily the stern necessity for labor. No man ever lived and worked, and was content to live by work, who was not essentially honest, and did not become every day more manly."

Carlyle says, — "The latest Gospel is, Know thy work, and do it. Know what thou canst work out, and work it out like Hercules." "It is not with the sword but with the axe that man must hew out his way to greatness."

Though Fortune has been called a fickle Goddess, she seldom fails to bestow the boon of success upon those who, when shut up to their own resources, struggle on with a determination and courage that scorn defeat. The battle of life is not a mere game of chance. Learning, wealth, and honor are but the sequences of forces as unfailing in their results as the physical laws of the universe. The foundation of every man's fortune or misfortune is laid for him and in him, long before he leaves the paternal roof.

The Northern farmer says to his boys, on the morning of the first snow storm, "George! you may go to the barn and yoke the steers, take the sled, drive into the woods, and get a load of wood before school-time." "John! you can take the horse and sleigh and go to mill, and return in season to carry the *children* to school." "Charlie will cut and bring in some wood for his mother. Now you understand, boys! Don't stop to play until your work is done!"

The boys spring for their hats — for which each has his own peg — and then rush to their work. George, the eldest — fourteen — after a severe struggle with the steers in putting the yoke on their necks for the first time, he gets the tongue of the sled into the ring, and starts for the wood. He enters the woods, and cuts down a tree, — but it falls the wrong way. — He looks for a cause, notices his notches, and perceives that the tree fell directly across the lower or deeper notch. He attacks another tree — makes his deep cut on the side where he wants it to fall. And behold it falls in that direction! Henceforth he can fell the tree in any direction to suit his convenience. Valuable practical knowledge has been acquired — self-taught — and "experience is the best schoolmaster."

Now his sled must be turned, — he must contrive to load the butt log — a rock maple eight feet in length. He cannot lift either end without the lever, nor place it on the sled without the skids. These he invents and makes. The boy succeeds in getting home a good load of wood. His muscles have acquired strength, and his mind knowledge. No obstacles or contingencies will impart misgivings to him in his next enterprise. Now he goes to school, and begins his task in mathematics and philosophy with a will. As he studies, he perceives the advantages which a knowledge of mechanical powers and philosophical principles will afford him in his future efforts to overcome obstacles in providing for life's necessities. By thus associating labor and study, the body and mind are mutually developed. In a few years he may build a ship, or guide it around the world. And if he should ever become a merchant, or enter one of the learned professions, his early experience will not only be of daily and practical use to him, but the strength of purpose, the power of persistent effort, the "backbone" it has given him, will render success in any department of life morally certain.

Slaveholders are beginning to see that the sons of poor white men in the South, who, by reverse of fortune, have been compelled to earn their own bread by the sweat of the face, are rising in the scale of intellect, and power, and would even now be ranked higher than their own sons, if personal merit were the only basis of honorable distinction. No honest, intelligent Southerner, who is thoroughly acquainted with the intelligence and business capacity of the different races in the South, will deny that the African is better qualified now to obtain a livelihood than the white man who rules over him, if both were left with only natural resources and the labor of their own hands to rely upon.

The mulattoes, especially — and they constitute a large proportion of the slave population, — are the best specimens of manhood to be found in the South. The

African mothers have given them a good physical system, and the Anglo-Saxon fathers a good mental constitution. They have enjoyed the important advantages derived from the education of various kinds of labor. The contingencies to be met and provided for, the difficulties to be overcome in their industrial pursuits, have made them efficient and practical men. Give them the entire possession and management of either of the Carolinas — and let the masters occupy the other alone,— and the experiment would not be prolonged many years before it would be settled beyond any farther controversy, that the slaves could "take care of themselves"!

VII.

NATURAL RESOURCES.

"A country, whereof here needs no account,
Where from the sapphire fount the crisped brooks,
Rolling on orient pearl, and sands of gold,
With mazy error, under pendant shades
Ran nectar, visiting each plant, and fed
Flowers worthy of Paradise, which not nice art,
In beds and curious knots, but nature boon
Poured forth profuse on hill, and dale, and plain."

MILTON.

THE South has been called the garden of our land. Its genial climate, and fertile soil, — its abundant fruitage, and charming scenery, have won the admiration of travelers, who have described it in prose, or celebrated it in verse. Of this we make no complaint. Nature has here been lavish of her bounties, — be ours the humble task of learning how they have been improved, — or if not, how wasted and lost.

My early years were spent upon a farm, and with its variety of occupation I have always been familiar. In my first excursion, therefore, into the interior counties of the slave States, my attention was naturally directed to its agricultural resources, the habits and practices of those who till the soil, and the different results following the application of slave labor from those which legitimately follow from free labor.

The Atlantic coast of these States is a broad, level table land, varying in width from one hundred to two hundred miles, and seldom attaining an elevation of more than 150 feet. It is said to be divided into three terraces, rising one above another as you go back from the seaboard, each one being distinctly marked by different kinds of plants and trees. But the elevation is so small as scarcely ever to be noticed without accurate measurement. The whole of it is evidently of marine formation, and was at some remote period submerged. The soil is not deep, and is entirely formed from the decomposition of vegetable deposits, upon a base of sand which everywhere underlies it.

The first terrace includes what are called the bottom lands, which have a deep, rich surface soil, formed of silica and clay loam, combined with large quantities of vegetable matter deposited in the freshets, which are very frequent in winter, and cause most of the rivers to overflow their banks. They extend back from a half mile to one or two miles from the rivers. Being situated so low as to be overflown every heavy rain, they are not much cultivated. A little Yankee enterprise would dike them, and thus easily convert them to valuable wheat fields.

FOREST TREES.

The table lands produce a luxuriant growth of hard pine, pitch pine, and yellow pine. All these species of pine are very valuable for ship timber, and vast quantities of it are annually transported to the North for that purpose. The hard and yellow pine are both sometimes found on the bottom lands, where they attain a mammoth size among the magnificent forests of oak that abound there. The large pine trees used for masts of ships are usually taken from the low lands.

The white oak, as well as the live and red oak, grows to an enormous size on the bottoms. This species—*quercus albus*—(called "basket" oak, in the South) is so heavy that it cannot be rafted green, and hence little of it is seen in market. The wood is tough and durable, and is used in making all kinds of farming utensils, carriages, and even *baskets* — from whence its name. In one of my excursions finding one of these trees blown down, I measured it. It was six feet in diameter at the butt, and four feet in diameter 80 feet from the root. The cypress tree, and sweet-gum are found in swamps or bottom lands. Both are often seen from four to six feet in diameter. The cypress is a light, soft wood, and is often used for making canoes. Boards and shingles are also made from it, and as it is easily wrought, it is a frequent substitute for Northern white pine for the interior finishing of houses. The sweet-gum is very heavy and hard when seasoned. It is the best wood in the country for keels of vessels, naves of wheels, or any purpose where iron firmness and tenacity are required.

These lowland forests present a beautiful appearance when adorned with deep foliage and enlivened with the variegated flowers of spring. But in winter, when denuded of leaves, the long, gray, living moss that grows thick and hangs from every branch, gives them a sombre and dreary aspect, far from agreeable. This moss is sometimes used for beds.

The reckless waste of these valuable forests of timber in the South is truly astonishing to a Yankee. The pine and oak standing on the banks of their rivers, so near that the axeman can fell them in — and so near the harbors that the chopper's blows can be heard from the vessels — are girdled and destroyed for no purpose but to let the rays of the sun in upon the cotton and corn. And whole forests of pine are frequently destroyed to obtain a "crop of turpentine." On the banks of the Altamaha, within a dozen miles of the old city of Darien, I saw all the pines "boxed" for a distance of several miles. The outer bark is all taken off, up eight or ten feet from the ground, spiral grooves are then cut round the tree, and near the ground a deep notch is cut into the tree, lowest on the inside, next the heart, forming a vessel in which to catch the turpentine. This process destroys the life of the tree. The timber is all wasted, the fires soon get in and burn up all the growth and the soil, and the lands are left barren and worthless.

Timber lands on the banks of that river and its tributaries, covered with large pine and oak, from twenty to fifty thousand feet to the acre, were in the market when I was there at one dollar per acre. Make Georgia a free State and these lands would be worth from five to twenty dollars per acre, and would not long remain unsold.

PRODUCTIONS.

Of the agricultural productions of the South it is unnecessary for me to give a detailed account. The great staple is well known to be cotton, which is the leading article among the exports of our country. Some account of the manner of cultivating this, as well as other crops, will be found in another chapter. Besides cotton, rice, sugar, and tobacco are produced in large quantities. Corn, wheat, rye, oats, beans, barley, and other grains common in the North can be raised as well in the South, and if cotton, rice, tobacco, and sugar, were not more profitable, and especially if they were not better adapted to slave labor, cereal productions would abound in the South more than in the North. Sweet potatoes are raised in great abundance in most of the slave States. The soil and climate are also peculiarly favorable for the cultivation of silk, which free labor would produce in great quantities, and to great profit. The culture of silk was introduced into Virginia as early as 1609, and in a pamphlet published about that time it was said that "there are silke worms, and plenty of mulberie-trees, whereby ladies, gentlewomen, and little children, being set in the way to do it, may be all imploied, with pleasure, making silke comparable to that of Persia, Turkey, or any other." But slavery was soon afterwards introduced into Virginia, and "ladies and gentlewomen" were above labor, and the slaves, being incapable of cultivating silk, were set to raising tobacco.* In 1703 the cultivation of silk was commenced in South Carolina, but failed for the same reason. Slaves could raise rice more profitably. It was also introduced into Georgia when it was first settled, in 1733. Like all new enterprises, success was not always uniform. But considerable quantities were produced, and being encouraged by bounties, it bid fair to become a permanent branch of industry. But slavery was introduced in 1749, and the culture of rice, and afterwards of cotton, gave it the death blow.

COMMERCE, MANUFACTURES, ETC.

The Southern States have all the resources for foreign and domestic commerce which could be desired. The principal part of our exports are from their shores. The materials for ship-building abound in unlimited quantities. And the numerous rivers afford facilities for extensive inland navigation. How these advantages have been improved will be noticed hereafter.

The South also has all the natural advantages for manufactures, in the abundance of water-power, and fuel, in the nearness of the raw material, and the facilities for reaching the market. Under a free labor system it would probably surpass the North. For some years past strong efforts have been made to introduce this business into the Southern States, in connection with slave labor, — but not with much success. In 1850 the number of hands, male and female, employed in manufacturing cotton in the State of Georgia was only 2,272,

* See Sparks's Am. Biography, new series XII, 231.

and the value of stuffs made $ 2,135,000. In 1852 the number of hands was reduced to 2,037, and the value produced not so much by $ 600,000.* In South Carolina the whole number employed in the manufacture of cotton in 1850 was 1,019.

In Minerals the South is also rich. Gold, silver, iron, copper, and lead abound, and also coal. At a branch mint in the northern part of Georgia there was produced in 1851 $ 350,000 in gold. Alabama produces coal and iron in great abundance. Iron and lead are found in the Carolinas. The gold mines of William Dorne in South Carolina yield over $ 200,000 a year, and the quartz-crusher it is said will increase the product to several thousand dollars per day. In North Carolina the annual yield of gold is nearly as large, and copper also is found in considerable quantities. In Virginia, besides the precious metals, there is an inexhaustible supply of coal.

It may be well to remember, also, that the slave States have more than twice the extent of territory included in the free States. In the midst of all this natural wealth, how happens it that the South contains less than half so great a free population as the North? I will let *Cassius M. Clay,* formerly a Kentucky slaveholder, answer the question.

"I propose to show to them, how it is that this million of citizens have been expelled from the soil by inevitable and inexorable laws. In the free States, a man upon

* Hunt's Magazine, May, 1852.

fifty, eighty, and one hundred acres (which last, perhaps, is the average of all the farms in all the free States), can raise, educate, and settle in life, a large family! Why? Because he has his manufacturer and merchant set down along side of him. He sells everything: nothing is lost: "many mickles make a muckle" says the Scottish maxim. But here in the slave States, in consequence of all our markets being distant markets, Charleston, New Orleans, Cincinnati, or New York, and through them the great world, we lose all the "odds and ends" which are saved in the free States. But the main loss is in the main articles of production, and return consumption. For instance, the citizen of Fayette sends a pound of beef to the city of New York: there it is sold for six cents; but three cents comes off for cost of transportation — the net proceeds are therefore three cents a pound. But the farmer living along side of New York, sells also for six cents; but that is the net profit as he has no outlay in going to market. He sells, therefore, for twice as much as we. Of course if he can live upon one hundred, we must have two hundred acres. Again, the articles which he gets in exchange cost him near one hundred per cent less than us; or one half of our income is lost in consequence of the distance of our articles of consumption. If, then, the free farmer can live upon one hundred acres, we must have four hundred! Any one can well see, then, that if we must have four times as much land to live here, as there, we must of necessity emigrate. But a home market can afford manures; and high price, and personal supervision, encourage "high farming," and the lands are continually improving. Freedom gives education, education gives science in cultivation, and increased product — more leisure — more science — and more population. But in the slave States the "shinning system" prevails, — large farms are necessary in consequence of distance of markets — large farms can not undergo the manuring system; the virgin soil of centuries exhausted in deposite, is worn out in slovenly, ignorant cultivation. In Virginia, and Maryland, and North Carolina, were good plains, and fertile slopes, but slaves have turned them into barrenness. The whites emigrated — drove out the wild beasts and Indians — cleared the forest; but once more the tide of slaves follows on; the result is the same. Barrenness follows in the wake of the slave. The broom sedge, the mullen, and the briar, pursue ever in his footsteps! Are not those who have desolated Judea and Asia Minor, and turned her cities and fertile vales into the abodes of wild beasts — where "the fox looks out at the window, and the long grass grows upon the walls!" — as criminal in the eyes of Nature's God, as they who stoned the prophets, and rejected him who taught justice, mercy, and love?

The towns are subject to the same laws of depression as the country; and neither in the field nor the workshop, is there any escape from the ruin of slave labor competition! There are two great data upon which the growth of cities depends: the number of consumers, and their productive, and consequently consumptive, capacity. For they are but the aggregation, for convenience of society and exchange, of all those persons, who expect to give the product of their intellects or hands for the fruits of the soil. A hatter sells to the twenty thousand people of the county of Fayette, one hundred hats a year: under the free system, when the population shall have increased to forty thousand, he will sell two hundred hats. At the same time his real estate advances in value as the increase of population. He is a thriving mechanic — he can not only educate his children, but set them up in the same trade with himself. The father sells to the fathers of the country, and his sons to their sons — and what applies to the hatter, applies to every resident of a city; so that there is no limit to the population of the city or country, until such time as the earth shall cease to sustain the inhabitants. And by manufactories, Massachusetts, England, and some other countries, sustain a higher population than their soil by agriculture could possibly support.

"Now reverse the case, let slavery be introduced, and immediately, as I have shown, two laws begin to prevail: the whole population, white and black, begins to decrease, and the productive power of the black is only half that of the white. The result is that the hatter, who at first sold one hundred hats, in the course of these events, now sells but fifty: he is a decaying tradesman. Just at the time that he needs more money for the education and settlement of his children, he has less than in early life; the profits of his trade continually decline, whilst his real estate declines also, until at last he is compelled "to pull up stakes," to use a common phrase, and move to the free States, where his consumers from the country have gone before him! And this reasoning is sustained by experience. Norfolk, in Virginia, was once the emporium of Eastern Commerce, but slaves have driven out her whites; ignorance and sloth have exhausted her lands; manufactures fail, and commerce fails with them. Now Norfolk is forgotten, and New York, and Philadelphia, and Boston, are great cities, and the sails of their commerce whiten every sea. The Virginia Republican says, "a little more than eighty years ago, the imports of Virginia amounted to four millions, those of New York to nine hundred thousand; in eighteen hundred and forty-nine, the imports of Virginia were two hundred and forty thousand, and those of New York were ninety-two millions." That is, the difference in the race, in less than a century, all the natural advantages being in favor of slavery, between a free and a slave State, is about sixteen hundred times in favor of freedom! Cities in slave States with the first tide of white population grow to a certain extent of magnificence; when the slaves come in, they become stationary, then begin to decline. Chimneys topple off, and go unrepaired — underpinnings decay — houses go unpainted — shutters fall to pieces — lights are broken out, and old cloths and pasted paper are substituted — all things indicate, that the city is constitutionally diseased with slavery, and hastens to its end."*

* Clay's Speech at Lexington, Ky., 1851.

VIII.

SOUTHERN AGRICULTURE.

"The axe rang sharply 'mid those forest shades,
Which from creation toward the sky had spread
In unshorn beauty. There, with vigorous arm,
Wrought a bold emigrant, and by his side
His little son, with question and response
Beguiled the time." MRS. SIGOURNEY.

THIS picture is rarely seen in the South, as it is drawn in these beautiful lines. The foreign emigrant landing upon our shores, tired of the despotisms of the old world, turns his back instinctively upon the South, and makes his home in the free States. There are about twice the number of men of foreign birth in New York that there are in all the slave States combined.

And yet the South is a place of constant emigration. For, as will be seen hereafter, the Southern mode of agriculture very soon exhausts whatever soil it touches,—if we except the bottom lands, — and the planter is driven by necessity to abandon his premises and begin anew. And though he plants the first seed that has ever been dropped into the soil by man, the same result follows his labors, — fertility is soon succeeded by barrenness, — and as he is driven about by this curse, he seeks new fields, and becomes a wanderer for life.

He travels through the woods to the spot where he has decided once more to "pitch his tent," with his family in a long cart, covered with coarse cotton cloth, drawn by mules. The slaves go before the family, on foot, to put up a rude tent for their reception. They build a log house for the master, and little log cabins, the size of "Uncle Tom's," all around the master's house, and within a few rods, for the slaves. He takes none of the slave children into the new field with their parents. They are not wanted there. They would rather be a burden than a service to him.

The large trees are then girdled, by cutting through the bark all round the tree near the ground. This process destroys the life of the trees, the leaves perish and fall off, after which there is little obstruction to the rays of the sun as they fall upon the earth beneath them. The deadened trees are allowed to remain standing in the field till they fall by decay, or are blown down by winds. Hence a cleared field is seldom seen in the South, as these large dead trees stand until the soil is worn out by constant cropping, when it is "turned out to commons," and the young pines, or perhaps a different growth, spring up again, and soon grow and thicken to a forest.

The small trees are felled, and piled up, to be burned. The piling is called the "log rolling," in which whole neighborhoods of masters and slaves are mutually engaged in rolling the logs together for the burning. The log rolling affords some amusement, and much hard work. The whites soon become as black as "cuffee" himself, as the fire has previously run over the logs and charred them. In this labor the master and man work together. They eat the "hog and hominy" from the same kettle, and drink the whiskey from the same bottle, enough generally to place them all on a level before bed time. After the burning, the plow is put in, which runs very near to the trunks of the trees, as the roots do not spread out near the surface, as we see them in the North, but run directly down through the sand to the clay, upon which the soil and sand rest.

The field is now ready for the seed. But as rotation of crops is seldom instituted in a slave labor system, I will describe the process of the cultivation of the corn crop. The field is lightly furrowed with a plow, then marked off crosswise by dragging a long rake with wooden teeth, or short chains instead of teeth, four feet apart. Thus by the drilling one way, and cross marking the other, the whole field is struck off into squares four feet on each side. One kernel of corn only is dropped at every corner of these squares, forming rows four feet apart, running at right angles, so that the plow may be run in either direction between the rows. The old "Virginia" corn, as the large species of Southern corn is sometimes called, is still raised in most of the slave States. The new fields produce from thirty to fifty bushels of this corn to the acre. The same field is constantly planted with corn, year after year, so long in some instances that it produces not more than four bushels to the acre. Some planters grow corn and cotton alternately, but, as the same properties of soil are required to produce both, this is not much relief to the lands. The cotton plant flourishes on dry lands, but it exhausts the soil more than corn.

Northern farmers cannot understand how those planters can *live* who raise only four bushels of corn to the acre. But this is easily explained to all who are acquainted with the *manner of living*, and the system of cultivation they have adopted.

"But," says an inquirer, "why do they remain on the old fields that produce only four bushels to the acre, while the new fields yield thirty bushels, and can be purchased for one dollar per acre?"

The only answer I can make to this is, that in the old worn-out districts many of them seem not to possess means and energy sufficient to remove to more productive localities. Those who are able, or more energetic, emigrate to new fields. Others remain where they are.

When the fields have been planted a few years with corn, the grasses all die out. The Northern grasses, such as clover, timothy, and red-top, do not flourish well south of Virginia. The indigenous grasses of the table lands are the slender "spire-grass" and "crow-grass."

Southern farmers do not replenish their fields with manure, and one result of this is that weeds seldom spring up to choke the corn. Hence in the old fields, the hoe is not used after planting. No labor is required, except to plow each way between the rows, until the harvest. One slave and one mule can cultivate fifty acres of this corn on this land. The plowing is commenced about the first of December, and finished by the middle of February, when the season for planting returns.

Two or three months are spent in planting,—which leaves time to plow twice between the rows before the harvest commences. If four bushels to the acre are harvested from the fifty acres as the reward of the labor of one man and one mule, every master who owns one slave and a mule can raise enough for his support. In some of the old counties, where this system has been applied for a long time, and nearly all the properties of the soil, adapted to the production of corn, have been exhausted, I have seen hundreds of acres of such corn. *All the "first settlers,"* who had sufficient energy, had fled, either to the cities to engage in other kinds of business, or to the woods to take up new fields,—leaving behind them a poor, ignorant, dispirited, shiftless population, inhabiting old, black, filthy, open, cheerless log huts,—exhibiting a greater degree of misery, wretchedness, poverty and crime than can probably be found in any other Christian country on the face of the earth.

After the soil is *entirely* worn out by this process, and all the dark, earthy, fertilizing properties have been exhausted in the production of corn, the white sand appears on the surface again, and those old abandoned fields, as you look over them, appear nearly as white with sand as Northern grass fields when covered with a light fall of dry snow in winter, with the long spires of grass standing up through the snow. Lands thus exhausted of fertility are worthless for a free labor system. There is no possibility of reclaiming them by subsoiling. There is therefore no prospect that a comfortable subsistence will ever be obtained from them again.

"The middle region of Georgia," says Colton's Gazetteer, "was once very productive, but owing to the oppressive system of cultivation adopted by the planters, it has become in many parts much impoverished. And large gullies, and red, barren hill-sides often meet the eye in places where once abundant crops were produced."

COTTON.

The Cotton plant is an annual one, very vigorous, and it exhausts the soil rapidly. It requires less moisture than corn, and therefore suffers less in the severe droughts of a long, hot season. The seeds are planted as early in the spring as corn, as it requires a long time to grow. The field is formed into beds by the double furrow, about three feet apart, and the seed is sown on the top of the bed, a few inches apart, like apple seeds in the nurseries. The cotton plant resembles little apple trees of three or four years growth, when both are seen in winter, denuded of foliage. The capsule, or boll, which contains the cotton, is an inch or more in diameter, and resembles, in color and consistence, the puff remaining from a decomposed apple or potatoe.

When the cotton capsule is broken by the early frosts the cotton expands and unfolds, appearing at a little distance like the full blown white rose. Its attachment to the capsule, when fully matured, is so slender that it can be picked off as easily as the leaves of the rose just ready to fall. The pickers take it in their baskets to the gin-house. This building always reminds the Yankee of the old cider mill, where the horse walked around on the ground, and the apples were put into the hopper in the story above.

The cotton-gin is a very valuable machine, of Yankee invention, for which cotton growers have expressed peculiar gratitude. Like most useful inventions, the gin is very simple in its construction. As you look upon it, it appears like a cylinder made of circular saws. But it is a drum of wood, about three feet in length, the size of the bass-drum used by bands of music, encircled with saws two feet in diameter. The saws are one-fourth of an inch apart, in a horizontal position, with teeth all looking forward, like the splitting saw. It is made to revolve with sufficient velocity by a single horse power. The cotton is brought in contact with this drum of saws by the receiver, which has one side covered with strong parallel wires. The saws tear the cotton apart, and draw it between the wires, which are too near together to admit the seeds, and they fall to the ground. The cotton is swept from the saws by a revolving brush, and is then ready to be baled for the market.

The volatile oil and ammonia of the seed render it valuable as a manure. After fermentation in the heap has destroyed its power to vegetate, it is often used for this purpose, being dropped in the hill with corn, and seeds of other annual plants. Cotton is the most certain and profitable production of all dry, arable lands in hot climates. And they plant the old fields as long as they will yield two dollars' worth to the acre.

RICE.

The "rice-fields" are principally reclaimed from lands

lying on the margins of rivers, near the ocean. Dikes of earth are thrown up around the fields to prevent the tide-waters from overflowing them. They are then planted with rice, in drills about one foot apart. The fresh water from the river above is then admitted through gates in the dikes until the field is entirely covered. The water prevents grass and weeds from growing among the rice, while the rice will grow under water. After the rice comes up and grows a few inches, the water is drained off to afford opportunity to replant, or thin out, as may be necessary. The field is then flowed again with fresh water, which is allowed to remain several weeks before the second draining, prior to the maturing of the rice for the harvest.

This last draining off of the waters occurs in the hot weather of August and September, which occasions so much disease and death on the rice fields at that season. The vegetable matter which has been decomposed by the water, when exposed to a hot sun, fills the atmosphere with poisonous gasses. The malaria thus generated, is diffused through the surrounding country. The African constitution resists the effects of it longer than any other. The absorbent vessels, whose office it is to take up whatever is unhealthy in the system and throw it off, act more efficiently in systems that perspire freely. Hence the negro, who sweats more profusely than the white man, wards off the fever much longer on the rice plantations. I am fully satisfied, from this fact alone, that the growing of rice in those unhealthy localities would be wholly abandoned if the labor of the colored man could not be obtained.

ROTATION OF CROPS.

To whatever cause it may be ascribed, the fact is too well known to be denied, that a "rotation of crops," on which the success of farmers in the North almost wholly depends, is scarcely known in the slave States. This is one reason why the soil in the South so soon becomes valueless. Without entering into any speculation about the matter, I will only say that where the labor is performed *for* those who *know* nothing about the science of agriculture, and *by* those who *care* nothing about it, — whose only problem of life is to ascertain by how little labor they can escape the lash, — I do not believe that the rotation of crops, the application of manures, or any other means of preserving or replenishing the fertility of the soil will ever be found practicable. The experience of a hundred years is demonstration sufficient.

And the converse of the proposition has also been fully demonstrated. Some of the old fields, worn out by slave labor, have been purchased by Northern farmers, and by free labor cultivation they have been reclaimed and raised to more than their original value. Lyell, in his "Travels in the United States," though he has generally taken without question whatever was told him by the slaveholders among whom he was so hospitably entertained, has nevertheless recorded some important facts, coming so much within the sphere of his profession that he could not be deceived. In 1841 he noticed some of these worn-out fields on the Potomac river, where slavery had nearly finished its work. In 1845 he traveled down the river again, and gives the following account of his observations:

"As we sailed down the Potomac, a landed proprietor of Fairfax county pointed out to me some estates in Virginia, in which free had been substituted for slave labor since I was here in 1841. Some farmers came from New Hampshire and Connecticut, and, having bought the land at five dollars an acre, tilled it with their own hands and those of their families, aided in some cases by a few hired whites. To the astonishment of the surrounding planters, before the end of four years they had raised the value of the soil from five to forty dollars per acre, *having introduced for the first time a rotation of corn and green crops*, instead of first exhausting the soil, and then letting it lie fallow for years to recover itself."

Not only are the sandy loams on the table-lands destroyed by the Southern system of agriculture, but the rich clay loams, and the high rolling lands, are ruined by the same process. This fact has been well noticed by Mr. Hildreth in his "Despotism in America."

"When tobacco is the crop, the fresh land is planted with tobacco each successive year till its fertility is exhausted. When it will no longer produce tobacco, it is planted with corn and wheat, till it will not afford a crop worth gathering. It is then *turned out,* that is, left unfenced and uncultivated.

"In the cotton growing States, corn and cotton are planted alternately, till the land is completely worn out. When its original fertility is exhausted, no further attempt is made at its cultivation. It is turned out, and the labor of the plantation is applied to new fields, which presently undergo a similar fate. Thus, every year, a certain quantity of land is given over as worthless, and new inroads are made upon the original forests. Agriculture becomes a continual process of opening new fields and abandoning the old."

The alluvion carried off from the inclined plains destroys great quantities of plowed lands lying on Southern rivers. The "side hills," on the margins of the running waters, after being flowed for many years in succession, are greatly exposed to the action of the heavy winter rains, and often, after the grass roots are all dead, whole fields are thus destroyed. Sometimes large fields of fifty acres or more which have been recently flowed are all washed off clean to the pan in a single shower. By this constant washing of the lands thousands of acres are annually ruined.

Another great damage resulting from this constant transportation of soils from the country to the coast, is the obstruction of navigation at the mouths of the rivers. From New Orleans around to Norfolk we have frequent accounts of the filling up of harbors with sand. Forty thousand dollars, I think, were expended to clear out the channel at the mouth of the Savannah in the spring of 1853. So much of the red clay in the subsoil of the high lands back in the country is washed off into the rivers, that the waters are colored by it until they reach the ocean. All over the South, in the old fields on the banks of the rivers, impassable ravines may be seen, cut through the soil as the water came down the hills, and the naked barren subsoil of whole plantations is visible from the same cause.

CATTLE, SWINE, ETC.

All the domestic animals roam at large on the ranges — commons — in Georgia during the winter as well as summer, except the mules, which are kept in the stables and used for plowing. The cattle become very lean in winter, subsisting entirely on the slender "crow-grass," and browse. Vast numbers of them die in the spring from starvation, or perish in the rivers. All along the creeks and water-courses, when the feeble old oxen and cows go down to drink, their feet sink in the miry clay, and they cannot get out. For miles together the boggy margins of the low bottom lands are bleached with their bones.

The Southern farmer derives very little benefit from any kind of neat stock except sheep. In the spring the young cattle grow fat, and are fit for the table for a short time before the hot season comes on. But they are seldom found in a suitable condition for beef, without stall feeding, after they are more than four or five years old. Gov. Troup told me that he owned oxen that had never worn the yoke, and from which he had never received any profit, and all he ever expected to receive was the hides when they should die, if his boys should happen to find them.

Some men who cut timber for the market work their oxen constantly; and sometimes others who use mules principally, when they want to draw a load too heavy for the mules, send the slaves into the woods to catch the wild "steers" as they call them all, no matter how old, — and with great propriety, — for they always act like steers when an attempt is made to subject them to labor. An incident occurred while I was there which will serve to illustrate the energy and skill exhibited by slaveholders in the accomplishment of their purposes, with the aid of mules and oxen, when they have no Yankees to assist them.

Mr. W. had contracted to deliver some heavy masts for ships to a commission merchant in the city of S. He sent his slaves into the forest to select and hew the masts. One stick was prepared, about eighty feet in length, which measured, after the sap was all taken off, three thousand six hundred and thirty-four feet, board measure. Seven pairs of mules were then harnessed, and nine pairs of wild "steers" were captured in the woods. Yokes were then made of straight sticks, and with small bows the cattle were fastened together in pairs. One end of a rope was attached to the outside horn of one of each pair, and a stout negro held the other end, to pull back when it was necessary to stop the team, — as the steers had not learned the meaning of "whoa-hish."

When the sixteen pairs of steers and mules were all attached to the wheels on which the mast was loaded, and everything was ready, word was given to start! The negroes halloed, and screamed, and threw chips, and bark, and clubs, — and a complete *melee* ensued. Some of the oxen pulled in one direction, some in another. Sometimes the load would move a few feet, and then suddenly stop. Then the "Cracker" whipped the negroes, and the negroes whipped the mules. The angry mules would spring and rend a trace. The frightened steers would leap and split a yoke, or break a bow, and then fly for life! The slaves seemed quite willing to endure the whipping for the sake of the frolic. While the Yankee spectator could not help laughing at the ludicrous picture. After working nearly three days, and whipping the negroes and mules half to death, the mast was drawn about one third of the distance to the river, which was only a mile, and then the project was abandoned! Four pairs of oxen, such as are owned on any of the large farms at the North, could have drawn it to the river in an hour. But it was left to rot upon the ground, valuable as it was, for want of sufficient force to move it.

The raising of wool would be very profitable in the slave States, but for the destruction of the sheep by dogs. This animal is the companion of the slaveholder, and many of them are kept to protect him from the violence of injured slaves, and to pursue them when they run away. The hungry dogs make horrid havoc among the sheep.

The wool is coarse, and is used with cotton in the manufacture of homespun clothing for the Crackers. Very little "factory cloth" is worn in some of the districts. The old spinning wheel and loom are still in operation. The Cracker seldom suffers pecuniary loss from too sudden change of fashions. He is doggedly opposed to innovation. The first pattern of frock coat and trousers worn by the country planters in the Old Dominion, is now the most modern style in central Georgia and the Carolinas. Even imported dye stuffs are little used, as the native barks impart the favorite otter color at a less expense.

The extensive oak forests of the South afford subsistence for large herds of swine. The pigs — like lambs — are marked in the ears, and are then permitted to run at large in the woods. The owners occasionally take a bag of corn on a horse and ride out to feed them, for the purpose of keeping the herds together. Masters who own good acorn lands furnish bacon to their slaves; while the slaves of masters who own none but pine lands, and cannot afford to fatten pork entirely on corn for their hands, seldom or never have the "*pound of meat a week.*" I knew two fugitives from South Carolina, one of whom said that he never tasted meat until he was seventeen years of age. The other, from the same county, told me that he always had meat three times a day, and as much as he wanted. The former was raised in the "pine woods," far from any river. The latter lived near an oak forest. There was no discrepancy in their testimony.

When the swine are to be slaughtered, the dogs catch them, or the butchers shoot them. The old hogs become very ferocious in the woods after being hunted. The tusks of the males grow to a great length. I saw one which had been taken from a wild boar, over seven inches long. They are formidable weapons of defense, as many a poor, luckless dog has felt, to his sorrow.

Beeves, also, are sometimes shot by the butchers in the country, as they are better skilled in the use of the rifle than of any other instrument of death. At Oconee, two men went out to kill a cow. One of them fired, and the ball struck her head, but not in "the right place," as the butchers say, and it only crazed the animal. She rushed through the fence into the woods. The butchers saddled their horses, called the dogs, and gave chase to her. After pursuing her all day, they finally killed her, about dark, several miles from home, but so far from any house that they abandoned the thought of saving the meat, and they returned home with nothing but the hide.

FARMING UTENSILS.

Perhaps there is no better test of the civilization of any people than can be seen in their agricultural implements. I had long known that nearly all the really valuable inventions and discoveries made in our country had their origin in the free States. But the leading interest in the South has been, not mechanical, but agricultural. It was not unnatural, therefore, for the North to excel in this respect. But since almost the entire interest of the South is in farming, I expected in this department to find some evidences of skill, and progress. But I was disappointed.

The "nigger hoe" was first introduced into Virginia as a substitute for the plow, in breaking up the soil. The law fixes its weight at *four pounds*, — as heavy as the woodman's axe! It is still used, not only in Virginia, but in Georgia and the Carolinas. The planters tell us, as the reason for its use, that the negroes would break a Yankee hoe in pieces upon the first root, or stone that might be in their way. An instructive commentary on the difference between free and slave labor!

The "Cracker plow" has no part like the Yankee plow, below the beam, except the left handle. This is made of basket oak, is about four inches square, and a foot long, or deep, below the beam. The lower end of this handle, which is faced with a plate of wrought iron, half an inch thick, is all there is that makes it a plow. The right handle is crooked, and fastened to the beam at the lower end and to the left handle, by a pair of rundles. It turns a furrow only four inches wide, but it is made to land about a foot. It turns the four inches over upon the other eight, and thus goes over the ground as fast as the Yankee plow. The holder of the Cracker plow has little power over the beam when the plow strikes a root, or a stone, as the base of the plow is only four inches square. Hence when the plow stops suddenly at a root or a rock, the impetus of the mule jerks the forward end of the beam down, and "Cuffee" is thrown up on the handles. It is a laughable sight to see a large number of boys and girls plowing in the new fields, where some of them are being constantly tossed up in this manner.

The harrow is seldom used except in sowing grain, and not often then. It is easily made, and more easily described, as it is wholly constructed of the *top of a tree,* dragged over the ground top foremost, having the limbs upon the lower side cut off to such a length that they serve as teeth in the harrow.

The ox yoke is a straight stick of hard pine, square hewn, about four inches thick, six inches wide, and from four to five feet long, — of equal size the whole length. It is not like the Yankee yoke, crooked down between the oxen, and excavated on the necks — adapted to sit easy and not chafe — having sufficient strength with the least possible weight, — and so constructed that the oxen can apply their necks and shoulders in the best manner to move the heaviest load, with the least brute force, and loss of muscular strength. A pair of oxen will draw twice as heavy a load in the Yankee yoke as in those used in Georgia.

One peculiarity in the Cracker's mode of traveling to market always amuses the Yankee. Instead of seating himself in his wagon, to guide the horse, the Cracker rides his horse, and the wagon comes along behind, jolting over roots, and stumps, and stones. I laughed heartily at seeing a Cracker with two sore-footed little negro boys, all on one jackass, with a wagon load of cabbage attached, following after.

IX.

YANKEE AND SLAVEHOLDER.

"Ay! gather your reins, and crack your thong,
And bid your steeds go faster;
They do not know, as they scramble along,
That they have a fool for a master."

O. W. HOLMES.

THERE are no bridges over the large rivers in Georgia, except where the railroads cross. There are numerous rivers, streams, and creeks in the State, but not sufficient energy and enterprise to bridge them. Colton, in his Gazetteer, says, "there is water power enough in this State, with eligible sites for mills, to manufacture all the cotton raised in all the world, and grind all the grain raised in the United States." So the absence of bridges is not because *bridges* are not *needed,* but because *men* are wanted to build them.

Large trees fall down across stage roads in the slave States, and lie there for weeks, or perhaps months, because it is not the *custom* to remove them. In many places the mail stage will meet half a dozen in a mile, and have to drive out into the woods to pass around them.

In the winter of 1852, I traveled a distance of sixty miles in Georgia, by stage. Half the time was consumed in fording and swimming creeks and streams, going around old trees, and through bogs. Three days were spent in traveling sixty miles. Two slaveholders were in the stage, on their way from the city to their plantations.

Just before dark, on the second day of our ride, we came to a deep creek where we found a mule team loaded with cotton, stuck fast in the middle of the creek. A heavy rain was falling, and the water, running swiftly, had worn a new trench through the sand in the middle of the channel, about two feet deep and four feet wide. When the forward wheels of Cuffee's wagon dropped into the trench, his six mules could not draw them out. The hind pair of mules were all under water, except their heads, and Cuffee could not get to the shore himself but by swimming, which was a very uncomfortable mode when the water was cold and the current swift. So he concluded to retain his seat on the highest bale of cotton, hoping for providential aid.

When our stage arrived at the creek, the *gentlemen* passengers left it and went up stream a few rods. and crossed over on a pine log. Two ladies remained inside the coach, — the horses swam across, — the coach filled with water, and one of the ladies was nearly drowned!

While stopping upon the other side, after "passing the Rubicon," another negro drove down with a mule and buggy, to cross the creek. "Billy," said the driver, who was a white man, and acquainted with the slave "you can't go through the creek. It is washed out deeper. You see how Cuffee's wheels sink — you had better go back and wait till morning."

"I must go through," replied Billy, resolutely. "Master told me to go up to the academy and bring young Master George home from school."

And he drove the mule into the creek. When the forward wheels of the buggy dropped into the new trench, Billy's mule fell over on his side and broke both of the thills. The whiffle-tree bolt was thrown out. The mule righted and swam to the extent of the reins, which Billy "paid out" to the end and the length of his arm, still holding them firm in his fist, as the only attachment between the buggy and mule. The mule "struck bottom," where he was "hauled to." Now there was Cuffee, sitting on his highest bale of cotton, in the water to his knees; and Billy, standing in his buggy, with the water to his waist.

"Come, driver, take off a span of horses," said I, Yankee-like, "and help the poor boys out." "If you want to go on with me, sir, get aboard," said the driver. I pitied the negroes and the mules, as it was now nearly dark — the water and weather cold — with the prospect of a dark, cheerless, stormy night before them, and no house within four miles. But what could a lone Yankee, who had no horse of his own, do for them, more than to pity them? Fortunately, another stage, passing that way that night, finding the creek blockaded with wrecks, helped Cuffee and Billy out of their trouble. We traveled on two hours longer, but only four miles farther, and reached our quarters for the night.

The next morning we started "bright and early." I had been talking freely on the way with the slaveholders about the "peculiar institution," expressing great astonishment at seeing so wide a contrast between the North and the South in everything relating to industrial matters. I remarked that at the creek, where we met so much trouble the night previous, there were noble pine trees standing by the side of the creek, long enough to reach across — that two "live Yankees" would fell a pair of stringers over, and cover them in a single day, — that no Northern farmer would neglect to bridge such a stream separating lots of tillage or pasturage, where he wanted to drive herds from one to the other, for a single year, while the Southern planter will ford the creek lying between his house and stable a whole life time. While engaged pleasantly in making comparisons of this kind, and extorting confessions from my slaveholding companions in favor of the superior enterprise and ingenuity consequent upon a free labor system, we came to a slough in the road. The driver leaped from his seat, and commenced pulling away the rail fence — "Virginia fence" — where the ends of the rails, at angles of twenty degrees, lock in and rest upon each other.

"What are you doing now, driver?" asked an outside passenger.

"I am going through the oat-patch," replied the driver. "You see the teams have balked in the slough, so we must either tote some more pine boughs and put into the ruts, or go around; and I think here is a right smart chance to go around."

I looked out upon the oat stubble, and being a farmer's

son, and acquainted with the appearance of surface soils in the spring time, when the waters have soaked the subsoil and made it soft and yielding, I saw at a glance that the slough extended across the field, and I had the Yankee impudence to administer a caution.

"Driver, you can't go through there! Don't you see it is soft out there? You are safer in the road."

"I am the driver, sir, if you please," was the caustic reply, in his Cracker tone of voice, as sharp and shrill as that of the overseer when he calls the "morning roll," or drives the "sugar-house paddle."

"Very well, sir," said I, complacently. The fence opened to the right and left, and the horses *shot in.* Their feet soon began to settle in the loam — the wheels began to cut through the sward — the whip began to crack — and the driver to swear and scream. The horses seemed frightened, and they snorted, and stamped, and pulled, and shifted legs, but not places. The wheels cut through the stubble and sank down till the bottom of the coach rested on the ground, and we were anchored. Still the lash fell, and the horses strove, sinking deeper and deeper, till it seemed that our only chance would be on the "underground railroad."

We "lightened the ship," detached the team, and after a terrible shower of curses on sloughs, and oaths on the fates, and gentle reproofs on the daring driver, had fallen from the eloquent, fluent lips of the passenger slaveholders, — whose dialect loses half its eloquence and all its grammar without the rhetorical finish of the cursing and swearing, the practical question,—"what shall be done?" was earnestly mooted.

"Gentlemen," said I, "this is a judgment upon you, for not helping the negroes out of the creek last night. Now, driver, you will please leave my trunks here. I see a house out there in the woods, and I am going there to stop till the next stage comes along."

"Oh, no!" vociferated the passengers, "that won't do! For if the *Yankee* leaves us, we shall never get out of this fix."

"I have no expectation that you will," said I, "for you don't know *how*, in the first place; and if you *did*, you would think it a disgrace to do the necessary work. I would willingly and cheerfully assist to get the coach back into the road again, but I am confident that all your plans and efforts will be fruitless; and so I have concluded to make the best of the calamity, and stop over to-day; although I must confess my regret at the folly which has caused the delay, as I am really desirous of getting through to-day, to meet a friend, by agreement, on important business. But I give you my opinion freely, gentlemen, that the case is hopeless, as the doctors say."

The driver was not a little piqued at the severe reflections my remarks cast upon him, and he said in a confident, swaggering, contemptuous tone, "I reckon we can do as well without your company as with it, sir."

"Not so," exclaimed the passengers. "We want the Yankee here to plan. If he leaves, we shall not be able to get away from this place to-day!" One asked the driver to invite me to help them,— others besought me to remain and assist them. I replied that I had no faith to work with them, and Yankees never looked on as spectators in such emergencies. "But," said I, "if you want me to stay, and the driver will consent for me to be 'boss' of the business, and you will all agree to do as I tell you, I will stay; and if we don't get out in less than an hour, then you may say of the Yankee, as he now does of you, that he don't know how to do any thing."

After a little *whisky* persuasion, the driver reluctantly assented to my proposition.

"Now understand me,"— said I, "as *master* of this business — when I speak to you, I shall not say 'boys,' as you do to your slaves; nor 'gentlemen,' as you are accustomed to be addressed; but I shall speak to you simply as men. The 'boss,' in Yankeedom, when he speaks to the operatives, calls bachelors by their christian names, but married men by their surnames, from respect to their wives. This is understood, I suppose."

All bowed assent.

"Well, then, now for the work," said I. "Billy!" — the name of the bachelor driver — now as humble as black Billy in the creek — "take Smith" — a wealthy commission merchant — "and go and bring a large rail." "Jones!" a cotton planter from the chivalrous kingdom of South Carolina — "you run out to the house yonder and borrow an axe." "Joe and John!" you take the rails from the fence and lay them down close between the stage and the road, as quick as you can." "Gilman!" — a lawyer —

"roll that large, short pine log along here. Well done, Billy! you and Smith have got a good pry. Run the butt end in between the spokes directly over the hub. Now raise the other end — higher! Roll your fulcrum under, Gilman! That's it; pull down, now! There she rises bravely! hold on! Run here, Joe, with that rail! Run it in under that hub on the ground, — farther in! that'll do. Slack the lever, men! Now place the lower end of the lever under the hub and bear down again. Good! trig up under, Joe! Halloo! here's Jones with an axe. There Joe, you run again and help John lay down rails. Come, Jones! cut a rail up into pieces. Sharpen the ends and drive them under the wheels to hold them up! Zounds! what cutting! Yankee boys four years old cut faster than that. Give me the axe! Now, Jones, see a Yankee chop."

One, two, three clips on one side; over — one, two heavy blows on the other, and a five inch rail drops in two. Smith's attention was so earnestly fixed on the chopping, that he let go his hold on the upper end of the lever, which sprang up with Billy, who was sitting on it astride — the lower end, which was under the hub of the wheel, being covered with oily, red clay, slipped out, and down came the lever, crushing Gilman's beaver hat, knocking him down, tearing the leg of Billy's trousers, and barking his shin! Gilman scratched his head, and Billy rubbed his shin, crying out as piteously as ever black Billy did after his had been kicked.

"What a piece of work! Now the wheel has dropped down lower than it was in the first place. Why didn't you hold on, Smith? If you don't act better than this, night will find us in a worse pickle here in the rain than we left the poor 'niggers' in last night.

"Come, men! raise the pry again! Dash the fulcrum under! down pry! block up! Now under the hub! Push under farther, Billy, so it won't *slip* again! Down again, all right. Drive under the short rails! Raise all the wheels in like manner! Now we are ready to run her back into the road. But it will be a hard lift to roll the wheels up on the rails. I will hold the pole, men! and you take hold of the wheels."

"I will hold the pole for you, sir," said Billy, politely.

"*I am driver* now, sir, if you please," I replied authoritatively. "Take hold of the wheels there, with the other hands!"

The lawyer, the merchant, and the planter took hold of the muddy spokes with their kid gloves on, and the word was given. "All ready now! Roll it up!" But "*no go!*"

"As many Yankee boys eight years old would lift more than you did then! You can do nothing lifting in that way, men! You must put your shoulder down to the rim, and both hands to the spokes, one on either side; and lift once, like *Yankees;* and the thing is done."

Smith dashed off his black broadcloth and put his shoulder — covered with a clean, nice, linen shirt — to the wheel. Jones and Gilman didn't stop to fling off the broadcloth, but seized a wheel a-piece. "All hold now?" "Aye, aye, sir." "*Altogether, then! There, she rises!* stick to it! Lift! a little harder! most up!

For your life now! HURRAH! the trouble is all over! Now roll back, steady.—Here we are, in the road once more!"

"Now we will pull the coach over the bog. Driver! you and Joe take the team up around through the woods, and by the time you get it on the other side of the slough, we will have the coach and baggage there, and the fence up. But dear me, what looking coats and shirts for gentlemen to visit their friends in!"

"Never mind," replied the gentlemen, "we give in to the Yankee."

During the remainder of the journey we talked together freely about slavery and its consequences. And I received many polite attentions afterwards from those "chivalrous Southerners," who generously acknowledged that a free labor system best qualifies men for the contingencies of life.

X.

PRIVATE AND PUBLIC BUILDINGS.

"Windows and doors in nameless sculpture dressed,
With order, symmetry, or taste unblessed;
Forms like some bedlam statuary's dream,
The crazed creation of misguided whim." BURNS.

IN the cities of the slave States there are not only many fine public buildings, but also many elegant private dwelling houses, surrounded with beautiful scenery, and fitted up within with rich and costly furniture. It is to such scenes that Northern visitors are generally introduced. Here they receive those impressions that are so widely disseminated in the North, — that slavery is usually associated with refinement of manners, a cultivated taste, and a luxurious style of living. It is not my purpose to question the correctness of these ideas, so far as they refer to city life among slaveholders. Nor do I deny that occasionally something of the kind may be found on the plantations, — though the instances are rare. My object in this chapter is to take the reader into the planting districts of the South, among the "Crackers," and show him their manner of living, — the kind of houses they occupy for private or public use, — and some of the external features of their domestic life.

About fifty thousand, or one tenth part of the inhabitants of Georgia reside in the cities. And the proportion does not vary very materially in the other States. Nine tenths of the population are therefore to be found in the planting districts, — though only a small part of these are slaveholders. The "poor whites" everywhere in the country constitute a large part of the population. I shall not describe their habits here so much as in some of the succeeding chapters.

It will appear to some as an exaggerated statement, — and yet an extensive observation in several of the slave States convinced me that more than one half of the slaveholders live in log houses. I confess that this was one of the most surprising facts that came to my knowledge. I was not expecting to see wealthy slaveholders in the country living in the old log house first built for the family when they entered the woods.

One reason why so little has been said and known of their manner of living in the country, doubtless is that few Northern men have traveled extensively there. And another is that many who have traveled in the South, have misrepresented their condition in order to gratify the feelings and flatter the pride of slaveholders, from whom they have received kind, generous, and polite attentions.

A foreigner, whose letters have been read with much interest, in describing the furniture in the house of a planter whom he desired to flatter for favors he had received, represented his friend as living in a large and splendid mansion, fitted up with expensive articles of furniture. After speaking of many beautiful and valuable articles about his room, he closed with a description of a magnificent candlestick furnished for his use.

"I am now writing," said Mr. D., "by a *candlestick* that cost *seven hundred dollars.*" But he did not mention of what precious material the costly candlestick was wrought. A slaveholding clergyman, however, who spake as knowing the fact, assured me that the wonderful candlestick was nothing more nor less than *Cuffee, holding a flambeau!* I have more than once written letters in slaveholders' houses when I was less favored than this foreigner, — having to hold the pitch torch in my own hand.

One reason why the slaveholder does not build a good house is because he knows that in a few years his fields will be nearly fruitless, and then he may wish to remove, and pitch his tent in the woods again. Nor do they take any pride in the possession of fine houses. The only pride of wealth is in the possession of men. When a citizen is to be selected for some public office, the only question asked is, "how many *niggers* does he own?" If a large number, the inference is that he must be a smart man, and well qualified for the office.

The most common style of building in some of the slave States is to construct two log houses, about eight feet apart, one story high, with one roof running over both, connecting them overhead, — so that they may pass from one to another in the attic, and have a cool out of doors entry under the roof, between the lower rooms. Most of these houses are built of round pine logs, in rough style, and so large spaces are often left between the logs that one can look in or out, without windows. Thus made, they afford little protection from the cold in winter, — and the inhabitants of Georgia, during the cold stormy days, or frosty nights, often suffer more from cold than the people of Maine.

The roof is usually made of rafters, having ribs pinned on them, about three feet apart, covered with shingles four feet long, which are split from the pine timber by the slaves. Sometimes no nails are used in putting them on. A small pole is laid over each course of shingles, which is fastened to the ribs by wooden pins.

These houses frequently are made without any iron for any purpose. Even the doors are hung on wooden gudgeons, driven into the logs, and fastened with wooden latches and green hide strings. They are seldom shut, however, except in the night. No matter how cold the weather, or severe the storm, the door remains open through the day. No tool is needed to erect abodes for the Crackers except the "club-axe" and the auger. The Secretary of a Fire Insurance Company in the State of Georgia, — himself a slaveholder, — stated to me that in his opinion two thirds of the residences of masters in that State were made of logs. And in the Carolinas they are, to say the least, not any more valuable.

The want of energy enough to procure an article so cheap, and we should say so indispensable, as window-glass, is truly astonishing to the traveler from the free States. These log houses are often entirely destitute of glass. They have wooden shutters to close at night.

10

The eye of the traveler in some parts of the country will not rest on a house that has a pane of glass in it in traveling fifty miles, though most of the houses may be inhabited by slaveholders. In one of the best farming counties in Georgia I found a man who had been located there a few years, who was a native of Maine. He informed me that when he went to that town, though it was the shire-town of the county, there was not a single pane of window glass in any building, — not even in the church, court house, or tavern.

This gentleman built for himself a house with two rooms, one of which his lady denominated her parlor; and she concluded to have a window put into it. A carpenter belonging to another county was accordingly employed to come and put in four squares of "seven by nine," for which he charged *two dollars*. "As soon as it was known," said the lady, "that such a great curiosity was to be seen in the place, all the children came in flocks to see the glass. And they really became so great an annoyance to me that I had the window taken out, and a shutter put up in its place."

The chimney of these houses is usually built on the outside. Sometimes it is built entirely of wood, about the size of common cord wood, piled up cob-house fashion, with the interstices filled in, and the inside daubed over with clay mortar. But uniformly the base of the chimney is built of stones, as far up as the wooden mantlepiece, and then it is topped out safely with wood, or boards, or oak bark. The fireplace is large enough to take in "a mighty big heap" of lightwood, which supersedes the necessity of lamps. The hearth is constructed of small flag-stones, resting on loose sand, not always in a neighborly proximity to each other. The oven is not an appurtenance of the Cracker's chimney, as the cooking is done in the kitchen, — which means in the negro huts. These cabins are not connected with the house by any building, or any covering overhead. The food is brought in, and the dishes are carried back, at every meal.

Court-houses constructed of logs are not uncommon in the interior counties. And though churches or school-houses of any kind are not numerous, a large proportion of them in the sparcely settled districts are made of logs. They are frequently found in solitary places, — situated far from any dwelling house, deep in the woods, with no road passing by or leading to them, except a few foot paths radiating from them in various directions through the dark, solemn pine trees, — and a carriage track describing all sorts of angles around the old logs. I have worshipped in rude log churches located in such spots, — having no window of any kind — no desk or elevation for the minister, — nothing to sit upon except a few, narrow, rough seats, on scantling legs, without any backs. And the preacher sat with the hearers, — and in any part of the house which best suited his convenience.

I am aware that an influential Journal has undertaken to show from the tables in the census reports of 1850 that in church accommodations, the South is superior to the North. But these tables can be made to prove no such thing, unless by distortion. So far as I have examined them they do not disagree with the facts which came under my own observation. The average *value* of churches in Maine is over $2,000 — in Massachusetts over $7,000, — and in the six New England States it is over $4,000 each. In North Carolina the average value is $500. But the value of the Methodist churches averages only $400, and the Baptist only $360. In South Carolina the average value in these two denominations is $700. In Georgia it is $500. But these estimates include the cities, as well as the country. If we look into the interior counties the result is different. In Irwin county, Georgia, the average value of all the churches is $81. In Ware county it is $56. In the county of Montgomery, the residence of Gov. Troup, an account of my visit to whom is given in this chapter, the value averages $40. In the old county of Tatnall it is only $6.50! There are ten Methodist churches reported in this county, the whole of them valued at $105, — being $10.50 each!

The paucity of furniture and books in the homes of slaveholders is most unaccountable. Even in families that possess abundant means to supply these wants I have frequently seen them living without conveniences of which the poorest Northern family is seldom destitute. Sometimes you will not see furniture amounting to five dollars in value in a wealthy planter's house. I have seen such houses without a particle of paint on the inside, or on any article of furniture. A few old oak chairs, made by hand, in the rudest manner, covered with deer skins or green hides untanned, — a hard pine table, unplaned, — a wooden poker, instead of shovel and tongs, in the rock chimney fire place, comprise the whole inventory. There is no closet, nor wardrobe. All the bedding is suspended on poles overhead, or placed on an open shelf against the wall. The wearing apparel is hung on nails or wooden pegs, all in sight. And yet you will find on the premises several hundred dollars' worth of elegant saddles, and costly rifles. And perhaps a thousand dollars will be expended for jewelry and ornaments to adorn the person and dress of the daughter, — but not five dollars appropriated for furniture or books.

The Crackers live almost entirely on corn-bread and bacon. So uniformly does the fare include nothing else, that "*hog and hominy*" are everywhere descriptive terms in common use to express it. And this is the case not only in the States which I visited, but the following paragraph from one of a series of letters published in the New York Times, written by a gentleman of acknowledged integrity, shows that in other parts of the South it is the same.

"At Natchadoches, Texas, an old town of ten thousand population, we inquired at five stores for flour, butter, and sugar, and were informed there was none of either in town. At Crocket, we inquired at seven stores and two Hotels for these, and for fresh meat. There was none of either in town. Corn-bread, with 'pork fry' and coffee, has been placed before us at every meal, — breakfast, dinner, and supper, — at every house in which we have taken any food during the three weeks we have traveled in Texas."

I was taken sick in one of the lower counties of Georgia, and I feared that I should die because no suitable food could be obtained for a person laboring under *gastritis*. Nothing was to be had except coarse corn-bread, and soft, ill-odored bacon, that no Yankee could eat even when well, unless he was half starved. Scarcely any two articles could be named more unfavorable to the billious diseases of the climate than the only two in use. But a merciful Providence, — in spite of "hog and hominy" — so far restored me to health, that I was able to ride on horseback; and I started for Gov. Troup's plantation, on the Oconee river, twenty miles above, on the old stage road leading from Darien to Milledgeville, — the Capital of the State. I called at the first house of a planter, and inquired if they had flour bread, or milk.

"We have none of either," was the reply.

I called at the next house, where the outside exhibited signs of more wealth and comfort, — but found neither. I asked the planter if he had no cows.

"O yes, sir," he replied, "I have a great many cows, but they all run in the woods in winter; we don't feed them now, and have no milk at this season. In the spring we catch a few of the calves and confine them in a yard, to toll up their mothers, and by giving the calves just milk enough to keep them alive, we obtain what we want to use in coffee."

I called at every white man's house — more than

twenty in number — before I reached the residence of Governor Troup, and inquired for these articles, and I was invariably informed that they had none of either.

About two o'clock P. M. I arrived at the Governor's house, and found him eating his dinner, in a log house. Having some business with him, I was cordially invited to sit with him at his dinner table. In addition to corn-bread and bacon, he had some dry ship bread, and corned beef. But instead of coffee, he had spirits of all kinds, of which he urged me to partake, on his assurance that that they were good; but when I gave, in excuse, my custom, and my feeble health, he ordered some coffee for me. He apologized for the absence of flour bread. He said the freshet had continued so long that he had been unable to get in flour over the creeks and rivers.

The upper part of a pig's head — "the minister's face"— was on the table. The ears had not been cut off previous to baking, and they were so very long, and stood up so straight, and wore a mark so singular, that I was probably eyeing it too sharply to seem respectful, when the old gentleman remarked, facetiously, —

"You see I am an honest man, sir, for that is my own mark in the pig's ear."

The Governor, like most of the large slaveholders, had been unfortunate in his sons. He owned, as I had been informed, about a thousand slaves, on different plantations. He had a large number on a plantation twenty miles below, which I had visited. His brother, Colonel Troup, was, as I was told, the overseer on this plantation for several years. He led a dissipated life, and found an early grave. I was told that he confessed to a minister, a few days prior to his death, that he had terrible remorse of conscience in the reflection that many of his own children would be left as his brother's slaves.

Governor Troup's eldest son succeeded his brother as the manager of the lower plantation, where he lived a few years in dissipation, and died from its effects. His youngest, and now only son, was sent to take the place of the first, and he followed in his footsteps. After being wrecked both in morals and mind, he was sent, as I heard, to the Insane Hospital, — and I suppose he was there at the time of my visit.

If the sons of his Excellency were as fine looking as any one of the bright boys I saw about his house, he surely had good reason to lament their untimely end. I saw no young men on that river who appeared so intellectual, and so highly endowed with natural qualities, as some of the mulatto servants in Governor Troup's family. They seemed devoted to his happiness, — but I ascertained that they fully appreciated their liability to a worse fate after his death, — as he was far advanced in years, and his only heirs were two maiden daughters, who would not be likely to keep the slaves together long after they should be left upon their hands.

Two of the whitest boys walked at my side as I rode to the gate, about fifty rods from the old house, — and I felt so deep an interest in their welfare that I took the liberty to converse with them in relation to their situation.

"You have an easy life here, boys," I remarked. "You are lucky to find a home so good as this."

"O, yes, master," replied one of them sadly, — "but we don't know how soon our master may die, and then we shall be sold away, and our lot may then be much harder."

"Well, boys, I would not borrow trouble, but would rather be thankful for so many blessings. You fare so much better than the slaves generally do, that you ought to be happy."

"I know that, master," replied one of them, "but still we cannot help thinking what we may have to suffer by and by."

"Well, be good boys, — don't drink whiskey, — take good care of your old master, — always do right, and you will be sure to fare the better for it. Good evening!"

"Good bye, master! good bye!"

O, how my heart beat for these noble boys! How I longed to speak to them of the blessings of freedom! What multitudes, alas! of these noble Douglasses, Bibbs, Clarks, and Wards there are in the South,—sons of Governors, Judges, and statesmen,—dragging out their weary lives in bondage! If some of "the best blood in Virginia" flows in the veins of the slaves, it is not less true of the other slave States.

XI.

THE PARTING SCENE.

"My God! can such things be?
Hast Thou not said that whatsoe'er is done
Unto Thy weakest and Thy humblest one,
Is ever done to Thee?

In that sad victim, then,
Child of Thy pitying love, I see Thee stand —
Once more the jest-word of a mocking band,
Bound, sold, and scourged again.

A heathen hand might deal
Back on your heads the gathered wrong of years,
But her low, broken prayer, and nightly tears,
Ye neither heed nor feel."

WHITTIER.

THE cars were coming down from the country to the city. I was sitting by the window, conversing with a wealthy, gentlemanly slaveholder, when our train stopped. Looking out, I saw a group of twenty-four slaves near the car, — some of them crying, — some weeping silently, — others running to and fro, as if in the excitement of incipient mania, or of approaching delirium, — while *one* sat mute in despair. The whole scene was so wild and unnatural that I did not comprehend it, and I asked the slaveholder what was going on there.

"Nothing, only some of these niggers are sold, I suppose, and the others are making a fuss about it," he replied, in a cold, formal manner, as he raised up his chin and gave a stoical, stupid look, and then he attempted to resume conversation with me.

Now had I been riding for *pleasure*, or traveling on *business*, I could not have written the history of this family, as I was obliged to visit the place again, and spend several days, to obtain the facts which rendered the scene at the cars intelligible. The whole family, including three generations of slaves, was there. This family consisted of the old grand-parents, with their six children, and eighteen grand children. None had been lost by death; and until now, none had been sold; and had I visited them at any former period of their lives, and proposed to offer them the boon of freedom, they would probably have refused to accept it, if by so doing they would have been compelled to leave their kind master, whom the afflicted grand-parents said they had always loved, as well as his father before him, — "in whose house they were born." But their young master had become intemperate, and a gambler. After losing all his money in the game, a few nights previous, he had staked six slaves — two boys and four girls — on a game of billiards, and they were won by a New Orleans gambler. The latter was putting them into our train of cars to carry them to S., forty miles below, where they were to be shipped for his own city, as I was informed.

I first noticed the old grand-mother, seated near the

car — sitting on a short, round, pine log, that had been cut off for shingles. Her emaciated form, curved spine, and snow white hair, gave her the appearance of being a very old woman. Her head was bent forward and downward, rising and falling as she inhaled the slow, full breath, and breathed out the deep, long sigh, followed by neither words nor tears. I likened her at once to an aged mother in a sick room, where a beloved daughter was lying upon a dying bed!

Her daughter was uttering the last words of affectionate, fond farewell to that devoted mother, — but she did not seem to hear the last words of her child. She was *beyond tears* — as physicians say — mute in despair! Or in the thrilling words of *Ida May* — "her sorrow was too stern and crushing for outward demonstration. The iron hand of slavery had seized her heart, and she seemed as if it were wringing the last drop of her life blood."

Next in order was the grand-father, an old man, bent down with toil, and bowed down with years, standing with the left hand resting on a long staff that ran above his head, and the right arm on the shoulder of one of his sons who was just to be removed forever from his sight. It was a vivid, life-like picture of an aged father, standing by the death bed of an *only, idol* son, on whom he had leaned for support and comfort in his old age, and upon whom he had depended to smooth his dying pillow!

A kind hearted slave girl in the neighborhood had taken the grand-children out a little way from the cars, where she was playing with them on the grass — just as

I have seen a kind neighbor's wife visit the house of sick and dying parents and take the children home, or to a remote room, to soothe and caress them, and thus divert their attention from the agonizing parent, and the death-bed scene.

The doomed fathers and mothers were standing with their arms around the necks of their wives and husbands, from whom they were the next moment to be torn! These mothers were, perhaps, to become the mothers of yet more unfortunate children in New Orleans. The wives and husbands of those that were leaving belonged on other plantations, and to different masters, who had kindly allowed them to come and take the final leave of their bosom companions!

Slaves usually have wives on other plantations. If you ask the slave the reason, he gives you this answer. "If I marry one of my master's girls here at home, I may never be permitted to leave the plantation while I live; but if I go off ten or fifteen miles and take a wife, every Saturday night my master will let me go to see her, and pass the Sabbath. In doing this, I shall pass by other plantations, and become acquainted with other slaves, — and thus there will be a little novelty, — a little more variety to life." This is one very good reason, and the only one the slave dare give, why he prefers not to have his wife at home, where he can be constantly present with her and his children, and where he can sympathize with them in their afflictions and sufferings.

But the true reason for this fact, which has few exceptions, is that the masters think it unwise to have slave families live together, where they can witness the punishments inflicted on each other. It has a tendency to make them discontented. And the same reason induces the slaves to conform to this custom. Their feelings are very strong, and if their relatives are to be punished, they shrink from the sight. And besides, they fear that if they should be present on such an occasion, they might interfere, and thus expose themselves to the same fate. Very few slaves can stand by, and look on passively, and see a *mother*, or *wife*, or *daughter*, or *sister*, brutally treated, by a lawless woman-whipper!

But the bell rings, and the slaves are ordered on board the cars. They break away from their wives and husbands at the sound of the whip — and start for the "nigger" car. One of them — whose name was Friday — bounded back and gave his wife the "last kiss of affection." Then the husband was pushed on board, and the wife was left! Friday's wife had a present tied up in an old cotton handkerchief, which she designed to give her husband as the last token of her love for him. But in the more than mortal agony of parting she had forgotten the present until the cars had started, and then she ran — screaming — as she tossed the bundle towards the car, "Oh, here Friday! I meant to give you this!" But instead of reaching the car, it fell to the ground through the space between the cars, and *such a shriek* as that woman gave, when she saw that solitary emblem of the fidelity of her early vow and constant affection for her devoted husband fail to reach him. I never heard uttered by human voice. It thrilled my soul, leaving impressions that will never be effaced till my dying day. Her heart was breaking! She could no longer suppress her grief, and for some distance after the cars started, the air was rent with her bitter lamentations, bursting forth with the most frantic wails ever uttered in despair!

There were thirty-five passengers in that car, but no sympathy was expressed for the wretched victims of the billiard table. Young ladies — daughters of slaveholders, well educated, connected with refined families — were in that car, but they did not seem to pity the poor, despairing slaves. They laughed at them, and ridiculed their expressions of grief. "Look out here!" said one of the young ladies at a window, to a school mate opposite, "just see those niggers! What a rumpus they are making! Just as if niggers cared anything about their babies! See Cuffee kiss Dinah! What a taking on! Likely as not he will have another wife before another week."

These ladies were returning from one of the female colleges in the interior, to their homes in the city. But sympathy for the slave is not taught in those colleges. I felt indignant, and so much did I pity the slaves, and so highly were my feelings wrought up, that I would have sacrificed my life, if that would have prevented the separation of those husbands and wives, and parents and children. I had remained silent for some time after the cars started, when the slaveholder said to me,— "What are you thinking about? — those niggers?"

"I will thank you not to refer to that scene," I replied

"lest I may say something that will endanger my own liberty."

"O well," remarked the Major, seriously, "they don't separate families when they can help it."

"Where are the children belonging to all the parents I saw in the droves recently?"

"O, I know," replied he, thoughtfully, "they have to sell sometimes, — but I tell you, my dear sir, that kind masters always avoid it as long as possible."

"*Yes sir*," I rejoined, sternly, "I understand now how you try to *avoid* the *necessity* of tearing the parents from the children — you ask for *more territory* to plant new fields in! Now sir, I will be most obliged if you will not mention this subject again, lest I might drop a word that you would deem *incendiary*."

We performed the remainder of the journey in silence. I could not safely have given utterance to my feelings.

XII.

SLAVEHOLDERS AS BUSINESS MEN.

"These base mechanics never keep their word
In anything they promise. 'T is their trade
To swear and break; — they all grow rich by breaking
More than their words; — their honesties and credits
Are still the first commodities they pass off."

BEN JONSON.

THAT slavery has had a disastrous influence upon business, and consequently upon business men, no one can deny. No fact has ever been more clearly demonstrated than that slave labor does not earn enough to pay its cost. Impoverishment and insolvency are inherent elements of it. And whenever we have had a general bankrupt law, the tables of mutual losses by bankruptcy, as between the North and the South, have shown a ruinous balance against the latter.

I do not deny but that there are many excellent business men in the South. It was my privilege to become acquainted with such. Many of these went from the North — but not all of them. And yet a regard for the truth compels me to say that the standard of business morality in the slave States is very far below what it is in New England. Business men are guilty of practices, without losing reputation or credit, which in the free States would prove their ruin.

As Georgia is a planting State, so the law relating to contracts is made for the benefit of the planter. The statute of frauds is common to most, if not all of the States. And yet in New England no man would retain the confidence of the community who should refuse to deliver articles sold by a *verbal* contract merely because the law would not enforce it unless it was *written*. The statute in Georgia requires all such contracts to be in writing, signed, and witnessed, — and five dollars to be advanced by the purchaser. But even after the stipulations of this law are complied with, where the party is not responsible, so that no redress can be had through the courts, written obligations are frequently violated by the lawless Cracker. He will sell his corn for a cent more per bushel, or his cotton for a mill more per pound, to any man who makes the bid after the article arrives in the market. So common has this perfidious practice become, that, in some of the cities the merchants do not send out their agents, but wait until the articles are brought to market, when, by bidding higher than the price at which they had been previously sold, they are sure to obtain them.

While traveling in the country, I purchased two rafts of lumber on a river, to be delivered in port within a specified time, at a stipulated price. One of these rafts contained a hundred thousand feet of ship timber, square hewn, and it was purchased of a county commissioner, who enjoyed the reputation of being one of the most substantial men in the country. I went to the port to await the rafting down of the timber. Previous to its arrival, a merchant in that city showed me a written obligation, which the same man had written with his own hand, by which he promised to deliver that same lumber to him for less than I had offered him for it. When he came with the timber I said to him that I was ready to take it, if he was under no obligation to deliver it to any other man. He said he was not. I then informed him that I had seen his written contract, and I consented that he should deliver it according to his first promise. He went out, — but instead of fulfilling the first contract, he found a purchaser who offered more than I was to pay him, and he sold it to him.

I purchased a thousand bushels of corn of E. P. Holstein, in Eastern Tennesee. Mr. H. wrote the obligation, and signed it, promising to deliver the corn to my employers at Savannah, within four weeks, at fifty cents per bushel. I waited until I suspected that he might fail to fulfill the contract, and I then wrote to him twice, requesting him to inform me why the corn had not been delivered. No answers were returned to my inquiries; but soon afterwards I learned that Mr. H. had been to the city of S., and had sold his corn for two cents more per bushel than I was to pay him.

I inquired of one of my employers, who was a native Georgian, — and a son of a slaveholder, — why it was that so little reliance could be placed upon the integrity of the Crackers.

"I know not," replied the merchant, "except that it is

the habit of the people. Any man will promise you any thing you want, and engage to do any thing you desire, without the least intention of fulfilling his word, unless it should be for his own private interest to do so."

"A friend of mine," he added, "who was intending to go into the cotton business here as a commission merchant, went out into the back part of Georgia, and a part of Alabama, and obtained pledges from cotton planters to send him eight or ten thousand bales of cotton. He came back much elated at his prospects for business, hired a store — went into it, and sat down to await the promised consignment. But not a single bale of the whole amount was ever sent to him."

I have written many obligations for the delivery of cotton and hides, not only by the Crackers, but by merchants in cities, situated in the interior, which were forfeited under similar circumstances. And I now have a letter from a friend — a commission merchant in one of the old slave States — in which he writes to me that he went into the country last season and purchased twenty-five thousand pounds of wool, and that, in every purchase, he paid five dollars, and secured the legal, written obligation. But after all his precaution he lost more than two thousand pounds of the wool.

I wrote to another friend — a slaveholder — residing in the country, expressing my surprise at the general want of integrity in the business men I had met with, and telling him of my disappointments and losses occasioned by their faithlessness. In his reply, he states, "I am not at all surprised at your disappointments. I have been here nine years to-day, and am just fairly initiated in taking lessons about the reliability of this people. It is perfectly agonizing to be obliged to carry on business with the laboring classes in this country. My lessons have cost me at least four thousand dollars within the last four years, — which is tolerably high tuition."

One great reason why business contracts are not more promptly fulfilled, is probably the fact that slaveholders spend so much of their time in amusements. These, more than productive labor, constitute the chief employment of that class, — especially in the new fields, where the fertile lands afford them the means of idleness and dissipation. No business is so important at any time as to prevent them from attending the horse-race, the cock-fight, or any other kind of sport.

I am acquainted with a clergyman who took a machine to a blacksmith in his parish, for repairs. While the smith was at work, a shout was heard over a cock-fight on the outside, and he left his iron in the fire, and ran out to see how the game was going. When he returned, the minister remarked that he was in a hurry for the work, to send away by the next train. Soon the shout was heard again, and the smith left the job a second time, and was gone until the cars had left. In his absence, his little son came into the shop, and took up some pieces of wood belonging to the machine.

"What are you going to do with those, Johnny?" said the minister.

"I am going to take them in for my mother to burn," replied the boy.

"O no," said the clergyman, "they are parts of my little wheel here."

But the boy, unused to any restraint, started for the house with the pieces. The clergyman caught him by the arm, and shook him until he dropped them, when he ran to his mother, screaming, and crying out against "the man who had pinched him." The mother carried the complaint to the father, who returned to the shop, and without asking any questions, knocked the minister down.

As soon as the clergyman recovered from the blow, he said, submissively, "I wish you had waited for an explanation, sir."

"I don't want to hear any explanation from you," said the smith, with a horrid oath. "I can flog my own boys."

The clergyman left the shop, with no prospect of obtaining the machine before another day.

When you complain of a slaveholder for not having a job finished at the time agreed upon, he refers you, complacently, to the time unexpectedly spent in amusements. A fox party came along, and he had to join that, — or the military paraded, which every body must see. I was employed to superintend the building of a mill, and fourteen hands were engaged six days in raising it, after it was framed. The dimensions of the building were only 40 by 70 feet, and the same number of hands at the North would have raised it in half a day; but the master workman took two of the hands and went off fishing a part of two days. The crew rested while they were absent. A squirrel ran by one day, and all the men left the mill, and chased him half a mile before they treed him. In this way was much of the time spent. Some of the owners of the property were on the ground, but I heard no complaint.

I attended the examination of an academy in Georgia. While a class of young ladies were reciting in English Grammar, two horses came up to the door, with a young gentleman on one, and a side-saddle on the other. The gallant dismounted, opened the door, and, bowing politely, solicited the company of the daughter of Mrs. J. to ride, at her mother's request. Miss J. left her recitation class, without asking permission of the teacher, and went to ride. Teachers at the South uniformly say that it is impossible to confine the boys to school so constantly as to teach them any solid branch thoroughly because the parents allow them to leave school at any time to enjoy amusements, which are so frequent that they occasion almost daily interruption of their studies.

If you charge a slaveholder with want of *honor* when he violates a promise, without any excuse, he retires behind the dignity of his fatal weapon, to shield his conduct. I asked the keeper of a hotel if he would furnish me with a conveyance to a county-seat, twenty-five miles distant, the next Monday morning, and he agreed to furnish me a team, and a boy to drive. As I had been frequently disappointed by this class of Southerners, I remarked to him, —"it is now Saturday, and I do not ride on the Sabbath. I therefore want you to be positive, sir; for if you cannot insure me a conveyance early Monday morning, I must go on farther to-night, as my business is urgent."

"You may rest easy, sir," said he, "you shall have the team Monday morning."

I saw his horse and buggy start off the next day, but I supposed they would return in season for my service. I waited patiently, therefore, until after breakfast on Monday, and then I said to the host, "I am now ready to be off with your team, sir."

"Well, father sent for my carriage yesterday," he remarked, carelessly, "and I had to let him have it."

"How is this?" said I, impetuously. "I thought there was a fair agreement between us, that you should furnish me with a team this morning to go to the city of D., — and I told you distinctly that I had business to transact there to-day which could not be delayed?"

"I admit that," replied the landlord, indifferently, "but when my father sends after my horse and buggy, of course I have to let him take it."

"Indeed! And do you think this is treating a stranger fairly and honorably?" said I.

"Why, you talk to me like I was a nigger, sir," said he, defiantly, springing to his feet and raising a hand to his pistol. Being a peace man, and having no weapon but a penknife, I did not utter another word of complaint. Saucy Yankees have to be very civil in the South, under such provocations.

The loose manner in which the public records are kept,

whether they refer to titles of lands, or private contracts, is a great annoyance to persons who have legal rights to maintain, and are depending upon them.

A neighbor of mine in New England had a son who resided several years in the flourishing city of Albany, in South Western Georgia, — but he was taken sick, and he died there. Soon after his decease, a merchant by the name of H. wrote to his father, stating that his son, who had died much lamented, had accumulated some property, and among his papers were found deeds of two lots of land in that city, besides other descriptions of property.

While I was in Georgia, the father sent me a power of attorney to settle the estate of his son. I inquired for the merchant who wrote the letter, and was informed that he was not living. But I found a brother of Mr. H., a former partner in trade, and inquired of him where those lots were located. He replied, that he was not aware that Mr. Varney — the name of my neighbor — owned any land there. I told him that his brother had so written to Mr. V.'s father, and I showed him the letter.

"My brother never wrote that letter," said Mr. H., "for he couldn't write his name."

I made extensive inquiries of business men residing there for information relating to Varney's property, but no one professed to know anything about it. I then repaired to the county seat, to examine the registry of deeds. But the name of Varney was not upon the records. I showed the letter to the recorder, and inquired what it meant.

"No doubt as it reads," was the reply. "But deeds are not always recorded here," he added, "as they are at the North. The State — for instance — when she sells her public lands to individuals, gives deeds to A., B., and C., and those deeds are recorded here. But when A., B., and C., transfer their titles to D., E., and F., they do not make new deeds, — but simply write their names on the backs of the original deeds, thus endorsing them as you do notes, and then pass them to the hands of the new owners."

In this manner are the titles transferred many times in succession, and many valuable estates pass by no better evidence of sale. Having learned these facts, I returned to the city and employed the ablest lawyer I could find to assist me. But after a thorough investigation, he said to me, — "I have no doubt there is foul play in this matter. Your deeds have been passed around through the hands of men who are determined to swindle your client; and I firmly believe that if you should find the lots, and should undertake to dispossess the present occupants, and claimants, they would shoot you."

Those lots are worth three thousand dollars, at least, situated any where in the vicinity, — but they could only be recovered at the risk of life. And I was obliged to report to my employer that the property of his son could not be recovered, and that any further attempt would be useless.

XIII.

SOUTHERN SPORTS.

"Then was all jollity,
Feasting and mirth, light wantonness and laughter,
Piping and playing, minstrelsies and masking,
'Till life fled from them like an idle dream."

ROWE.

THE slave States are proverbial for their amusements. The families of wealthy slaveholders are seldom taught to labor, or to engage in any kind of business. Life is to them but a play-day, and the question of every morning is — how to kill time? It hangs like a dead weight upon their hands. An old proverb says — "an idle brain is the devil's workshop." And the most prolific source of the drunkenness, licentiousness, and crime, which abound in the South, is in the idleness of the slaveholding class. Young men and young women have nothing to do, — and the theater, the billiard table, the drinking saloon, the horse race, the cock fight, are but so many ways devised to banish *ennui*, and prevent life from being a burden.

One of the most frequent amusements in some parts of the South is "*Gander pulling*." Two important branches of education in the "Peculiar Institution" —

gambling and fighting — are rapidly advanced in connection with this amusement. More solid, *personal* instruction is often *practically* demonstrated to students in these sciences, at a single exhibition, than is obtained by a whole college course in New England. And these branches of education partake so much of the graceful, ornamental, and indispensably useful learning in the polite, chivalrous South, that the "*Gander-pulling*" is patronized by all who walk in the fashionable circles.

I was at Milledgeville, the capital of Georgia. It is not a city of any great note, though it contains some fine residences. It is situated on the Oconee river, which below this point was once navigated by small steamers. The population is about 3000, and the inhabitants would consider it slanderous if I should say that any more polished or refined could be found in the Southern States.

Walking in the suburbs, I saw, nailed to the pine trees, large notices of the time and place for a Gander-pulling; and circumstances favored my desire to witness it. Word had gone into the country, and out among the Crackers, far and near. At the appointed time, rude whisky tents, and festive seats, and shades, were prepared around the "*pulling course;*" and thousands of spectators — ladies as well as gentlemen, the *elite* as well as the vulgar — assembled to engage in or witness the favorite sport.

The gander — a noble specimen of the wild goose species — captured for the occasion — had a very long neck, which was large as it rose above the breast, but tapered gradually for more than half the length, until it became small and serpent-form, terminating in a long, slim head, and peaked bill. The head and neck were lubricated with oil. The legs were tied together by a small cord, and the gander was then raised by the cord about ten feet from the earth, and suspended from the limb of a tree. In this position, he was for a long time the *hero*, but at last the *victim* of the sport.

Tickets were issued by the *proprietor* of the gander, at fifty cents each, to all *gentlemen* present who wished for them, and they entered their names as "*pullers*." The pullers were to start about ten rods from the gander, on horseback, riding at full speed, and as they passed along under the gander, they had the privilege of pulling off his head — which would entitle them to the additional privilege of eating him. A "nigger," with a long whip in hand, was stationed on a stump, about two rods from the gander, with orders to strike the horse of the puller as he passed by.

Now it will be recollected that fifty cents was a fair price for the gander after he was killed, and picked, and ready for the cook. So that the owner could well afford to sell a *single chance* to pull off the head for the *full value of the fowl.* Still, "*pullers*" were plenty.

One entered the list — a "gentleman of property and standing" — and dashed over the course. The poor old gander — seeming quite resigned to his fate, or not comprehending his danger, and not knowing how to "*dodge*" — had his neck seized by the first rider; but being well oiled, and his head so small, and his strength not yet exhausted, he slipped his head through the puller's hand without suffering much from the twist. But he drew up his head — as he saw the next puller coming — looking wise and shrewd, as much as to say — "you won't catch this bird napping again!" Still, unskilled in *dodging*, the gander's head was caught again, — but he pulled it out a second time, after a terrible wrench. After this he kept a sharp look out, and many pullers passed by without being able to grapple his neck. The game went on, and the pullers increased, till the jaded gander could elude their grasp no longer. An old Cracker — with a sandpaper glove on — pulled off his head at last, amid the shouts of a wondering host of intoxicated competitors.

This may be called the introductory exercise. The whisky kegs on the stumps — the gaming tables under the shades — the cock-fights in the pens — the horse-race out in the woods — will amuse the crowd to-morrow. And the fox-chase, and perhaps a nigger-hunt, will close the festivities.

In the morning of the second day, a luckless youth, who had lost his purse at billiards, brought the winner up before Judge W. for gambling. The Judge said that so many prosecutions for graver offences were already entered for trial before him, that he must put over that case till the next morning. That evening the Judge, dressed in disguise, passed through the gambling saloons, and swept the stakes, pocketing all the money in the crowd. The next morning he advised the unfortunate complainant to dismiss his complaint against the person charged with gambling, as he had an assurance that there would be no more offences of the kind; and therefore he thought it best to stop without farther proceedings.

That night, at two o'clock, the landlord came to my door and rapped, saying that his house was full, and a gentleman who had often stopped there had called to lodge; but his beds were all taken up, and he desired that I would allow his old friend to take lodgings with me in my bed, as otherwise he would be under the unpleasant necessity of turning him off.

"If you *know* him to be in reality a *gentleman*, sir," said I, "I will consent, from a regard to your wishes and feelings, that he may share the bed with me *to-night*, hoping that the favor will not be solicited of me again while I remain at your house."

"Thank you, sir," added Mr. J. "You may be assured, sir, that I would not ask you to take in a companion, if I were not well acquainted with him, and did not know him in every respect to be an honorable gentleman."

"Very well, sir," said I, "you may invite him up here on your own certificate."

I unbolted the door, and the stranger walked in with a very graceful bow, and a bland "good evening, sir."

"Good *morning*, sir," said I.

"It is too early yet for me to say *morning*," he replied, "as I usually make later evenings than this."

I remained silent after this remark while my chum threw off his dress, from which he detached a bowie knife and pistols, — laying the knife and one pair of the pistols on the table, and placing another pair under his pillow. I shuddered — having never slept with pistols — but I composed my nerves with the landlord's assurance of a favorable acquaintance, and the historical fact that *Southern* "gentlemen" sleep with pistols. The light was extinguished, and the stranger laid himself down at my side. At once he asked several familiar questions, inquiring where was my residence, and what was my occupation, &c., — to which full and explicit answers were given; and to be as polite in return, I inquired what his *profession* was, — inferring from his style of expression that he was a literary gentleman, who was probably well read in some one of the learned professions — when to my surprise he informed me that he was "a gambler *by profession*."

Now, by the way, gambling is an open profession in that locality, and is regarded as honorable and as respectable as the profession of law or medicine; but I had a different education, and was agitated a little with fear, but more with indignation, when my bed-fellow told me that he was a gambler.

"The landlord assured me that you were a *gentleman*, sir," said I to him, "but had he told me of your profession, I would not have consented for you to share my bed."

"Why not?" asked the gambler, complacently. And he entered into an elaborate argument to prove that his profession was as honest and honorable as that of the physician.

It is customary in the South, after a warm day, to

have speeches made in the evening under the awnings and piazzas, or on the walls and in the parks in the cities, and wherever men congregate at night around the taverns and liquor shops in the country.

In April, 1853, I was stopping, with a friend of mine from Massachusets, in the old city of Darien — of which I shall give some account in the next chapter. It was a beautiful evening, and as a crowd was standing around the hotel, Capt. L., a Custom House officer in that port, having some acquaintance with us, called for speeches "from the Yankees."

"My friend here, Mr. W.," said I, "is an abolitionist, so that it will not answer for him to make an abolition speech; but if he will make a temperance speech, I will give you an abolition speech."

"Good!" ejaculated Capt. L., "let us have them!"

My friend made a neat, appropriate temperance speech, in no respect offensive to the wine-bibbers and whisky-soakers present, and then I gave them my abolition speech, stating simply such facts as had come to my knowledge, mostly from personal observation.

"Gentlemen!" said I, "the amount annually paid into the post-office department by the slave States is less by about half a million dollars than the cost of supporting it in these States. This deficiency is principally paid by the North. I understand now, gentlemen, the causes which have rendered you unable to sustain your own mails. I have been traveling among the Crackers, in the "old fields," where I find that the people cannot read and write. Of course little matter passes through the mails to them. I was at the post-office at D., up here in the valley of the Altamaha, where slavery was first applied, and where it has nearly finished its work. I inquired of the post-master, on the seventh day of February, whether a letter would come to me at that place from Jacksonville, Florida, across the country, sixty-five miles, or would be carried around on the railroad, and be brought down river by stage to that place.

'I think,' said the post-master at D., 'that your letter will come down from the railroad, — for the mail-carrier from Jacksonville has not been up here since last fall."

'Since last fall?' said I.

He afterwards confessed that the manner in which I put the second question, left the impression on his mind that the post-office department had sent me there to inquire into the particulars in regard to that mail route, and he began to make explanations, and to apologize for his friend, the mail-carrier.

'I remember,' said he, 'that he came up once or twice without a letter or a paper. He is a very faithful, honest man, sir, and you may be assured, that if there was any thing to bring, he would forward it promptly.'

'I should like to know when he was last here,' said I.

'I will inform you, sir,' he replied.

He looked at the books and showed me the record, giving the last date of the receipt of mail matter by that route, from Jacksonville, which was on the eleventh day of the October previous; making four months, wanting four days.

'Do you know what they pay him for carrying this mail?' said I.

'Six hundred and fifty dollars, I believe,' he answered.

Again, gentlemen, I was at Emmett, on the central railroad leading from Savannah to Macon, when the mail was opened, and behold! two letters only were left at that office on that day. One of these was addressed to me, and the other to another Yankee, who was passing that way. I had no reason to complain, as I had half the mail.

They have post-offices at every station, ten miles apart, on that road, but so little matter is left at those offices, that the passenger train stops while the mail is assorted. There are twenty post-offices on that road of two hundred miles, but only one school house and one church to be seen as you ride over it. These post-offices are established for the accommodation of a few planters, who send their cotton to the different stations.

A merchant belonging to South Carolina gave me an account of the burning of abolition papers in the city of C. Some suspicions were entertained that such documents were received at that post-office, and a select company of merchants went to the office and demanded the mail for an examination. The post-master would not consent to have the mail taken out and examined for that purpose.

'If you don't give us the papers,' said one of the merchants, 'we will burn the office down, sir.'

'I will be absent about three o'clock this evening, gentlemen,' responded the postmaster, timidly.

'We went to the office at three o'clock,' said my informant, 'and found the post-master absent—but the key was in the door, and we walked in. By a careful looking over, we found a few abolition documents, and one newspaper, and some two or three letters, that we marked *incendiary,* and then we took them out into the street. The pile was too small to make a fire worth looking at when the sun was shining, and we bought a bale of poor cotton — *dog tail* — for which we paid fifteen dollars, tied the inflammatory papers to it, and got up a respectable bonfire!' "

I thus carried my remarks quite as far as was prudent, and continued speaking until I noticed that some of my auditors began to look excited and angry, — querying whether I was indeed one of the fanatics, and evidently surprised that I should dare to repeat such facts, with so much earnest sincerity and independence. Capt. L., however, came to my relief, by diverting the attention of the crowd. "Now," said he, "I will tell you of a frolic we had catching an abolitionist!" And assuring the listeners that it was safe to give me the facts, inasmuch as they knew some of my friends in that State who were true to the South, he proceeded to relate substantially the following amusing story.

In the autumn of 1852, a gentleman from New York came to Darien, and took lodgings at the same hotel where we were stopping, entering his name on the register as a Mr. Smith. He was a very fine looking man, large, tall, handsome, and elegantly dressed in black. He always appeared dignified and grave, did not drink or swear, or even seem to be light minded. After he had boarded there a few days, Capt. L. asked him if he was a clergyman. He replied, very politely, that he was not. The next morning he put his trunks on the stage, directed to Macon, and after taking breakfast, he called for his bill, paid it, and started off up river on foot, about an hour after the stage had left.

Capt. L. then inquired of the landlord why that gentleman had left in that manner, when he appeared as though he had the means of traveling respectably. The landlord said he knew nothing about the gentleman, or about his business. Then they sent the niggers all around to the stores, and wharves, and lumber yards, to inquire what Mr. Smith's business had been in the city. But no information was obtained. They called on the landlord again, and inquired if Mr. Smith had brought with him any reference from any bank, or commercial house, or testimonials from any reliable source.

"He did not show me any papers of the kind," replied the landlord. "His conduct, in my house, so far as I know, was perfectly correct and gentlemanly. I knew nothing about him, except that he was out late at night. The niggers had to be up till two or three o'clock, sometimes, to let him in."

Out late nights! What in the world could a *gentleman* be doing out so late at night in that city? They once had a gambling house, but it had been run down so low since the cotton trade fell off, that that haunt had been abandoned. This Mr. Smith, moreover, had exhibited no characteristics of the gambler's profession in his deportment or conversation. So the inference was, that he must be an *abolitionist*. This at once explained his conduct. He was out to the nigger huts in the night, either planning an insurrection, or preparing to take some of them North. The alarm ran through the old city like wildfire. So much life had not been seen for years. A large crowd soon gathered to commence proceedings in the case. The city marshal, Mr. C., who was present, was ordered to pursue Smith and bring him back to the city for public examination. The marshal, however, said he would not go alone, but would go if the Custom House officer would accompany him. Capt. L. was ready to go, but not without more attendants than the marshal, as he was small, and the abolitionist was a large, stout man, with a stalwart arm, and was no doubt well armed; but if a sufficient number of gentlemen would volunteer to go to make it perfectly safe, they would start. Ten others at once volunteered. The horses were brought out, and, all armed, booted, and spurred, they dashed away in hot pursuit of the mysterious stranger. They overtook Smith, who was walking very fast, within one mile of Fort Barrington, fourteen miles from the city.

They all rode by, dismounted, tied their horses, and then formed a solid phalanx across the road. As the abolitionist drew nigh, the marshal advanced a few steps towards him, and arrested him. Smith threw up his hands in consternation, and exclaimed, "what does this mean?" looking as frightened as he would, had he known that he was to be shot the next instant.

"You must go back to the city," said the marshal, "and you will find out there what it means."

"But what have I done in the city, sir," asked Smith,

trembling in every joint, "that you have come out against me in this manner?"

"We have no time to parley with you," replied the marshal. "Put about, sir!"

"Have you a warrant against me?" inquired Smith, looking as pale as death.

"No," answered the marshal, "we had not time for that; but our orders are, to take you back; so we will bandy no more words about it."

"Grant me one favor," said Smith. "I have promised to be at M.,—which is more than two hundred miles distant,—in one week; and being about out of money, I am obliged to travel on foot. And now, sir, will you be so kind as to tell me what your suspicions are in relation to me?"

After much persuasion, the marshal informed him that they *suspected* he was an *abolitionist.* Then, his face brightening up, and the load seeming to fall from his shoulders, he exclaimed, "Heaven knows, gentlemen, that I am no abolitionist! I am a gambler. I was out late nights, looking for some chance to follow my profession; but you have run down there so, that I could find no gambling house,—and as my pockets were nearly empty, I was obliged to leave in this manner."

"Fudge!" rejoined the marshal, "you can't deceive us in that manner. *Search him, boys!*"

And the volunteers took off his hat and coat, threw him down and pulled off his boots and pants, and searched every part of his dress to see if they could find any abolition documents on his person. But nothing of the kind was found. Still the marshal insisted that Smith must go back to the city, for such was the direction that he had received from the *authorities*.

"Well, I will tell you what I will do, gentlemen," said Smith. "I have only nine shillings left; but if any of you will risk a game with me, I can give you ocular demonstration that I am what I profess to be — a gambler."

"Now we were all gamblers," said Capt., L., "and, we thought, as shrewd as could be found any where; and so we readily accepted the challenge. Down we sat in the woods, and commenced the game. And in less than an hour, the abolitionist got every shilling of money there was in the crowd! He was, however, a noble, generous, magnanimous fellow. He took us to the tavern at B., and gave us some good brandy, and a good dinner, after which we came home, and let the stranger go on his way rejoicing. But when we got back to the city, you never saw a pack of fellows so ashamed as we were, to find the whole city paraded in the streets to receive us, and hear our report!"

While Capt. L. was relating this story, I could not help thinking of my own condition at that time. My note book was in my pocket, and in my trunk might have been found abundant evidence of my abolitionism. I confess I was not without my fears. And since my return to the North, especially when reading accounts of men being mobbed in the South for their anti-slavery sentiments, I have often wondered that I escaped. But I have no doubt the well known fact that I had relatives who were slaveholders, was a protection to me. And I think also, as strange as it may appear, that the freedom with which I expressed my views allayed the suspicions of those with whom I conversed. They look upon a real abolitionist as a *secret* enemy — one who comes in disguise, and endeavors to incite the slaves to insurrection or desertion. But while I always frankly expressed my opinions, there was nothing in my conduct which could lead them to suspect me of any such designs. I was at all times on intimate terms with slaveholders, and that class of persons who do the work of mobs — who seldom own slaves themselves — were respectful towards me, probably for that reason.

XIV.

TREATMENT OF SLAVES.

"Sad and weary — all forlorn —
Slaves must work from early morn;
Drear the day, and dark the night, —
Woes of slaves find no respite.
Though I toil, I nothing gain,
Joy ne'er comes to pay for pain."

NEGRO MELODY.

MY object in giving some account of the treatment of slaves, is not to draw from it an argument against the system. If slaves were always treated kindly, it would by no means justify the institution of slavery; — nor does the fact that they are sometimes treated cruelly, necessarily prove it wrong. The child may be abused by the parent, or lawful guardian, — while the kidnapper may sometimes manifest the kindest regard for the physical comfort of his victim. And yet the actual condition of the slaves, as it respects their bodily necessities, and the treatment they receive from their masters and overseers, is a subject on which there is much interest; and the facts which came under my own observation were such as are well adapted to awaken our sympathies in their behalf.

In the northern slave States, where corn and bacon are abundant and cheap, the slaves suffer little from hunger compared with what they suffer farther South, where cotton, sugar, and rice, are more profitable crops. The slaves in Virginia have twelve quarts of corn a week, besides a small allowance of fish, or meat. In the States further South, the allowance is only eight quarts a week, and no more than this is allowed to those who have no meat. This is the quantity usually dealt out to about one fourth part of the slaves in Georgia, so far as I could ascertain. There is no regular, uniform system adopted throughout the State, however. Neighborhoods have their own conventional rules. In some parts of the State several contiguous plantations may be found where the slaves are not tasked or allowanced; where they fare just as well in respect to food and clothing as the masters. Such masters go to the field, plan their own work, and, if need be, help do it, — and they treat their slaves as kindly as they can safely be treated. But if you pass over a creek, or a river, into another neighborhood, you will find a different system. The task of "one acre a day," at hoeing, must be performed. The slave is put on allowance, and rigorously treated in every respect. And it is sufficient to say that there is the same difference among individuals and neighborhoods, in the treatment of slaves, that there is in other respects. And men, and communities, differ in the South, as they do in the North, — though not in the same degree. For while freedom is the parent of life, which everywhere exhibits itself in boundless variety, — the tendency of slavery is to depress everything to one common level.

Some masters, who have oak lands, provide meat for their slaves, three times a day, and as much as they want. Others give them meat twice a week only; — others, none at all.

Slaves uniformly fare the hardest on the large plantations. I suppose it is really impossible to furnish meat to a large number of hands, on the rice and sugar fields, in the hot season. Salted meats soon become tainted, and fresh cannot be obtained. Some of the rice planters informed me that they had substituted rice for corn, in feeding their hands, but they were not so healthy as when fed on corn.

I spent a few days near a large plantation in the country, whose owner had five hundred slaves; and I had free access to their huts. They were never required to labor hard, as the master only desired to make the plantation support itself. His only profit was the increase of the slaves, which amounted sometimes to twenty-five thousand dollars a year. But though the slaves were not overtasked, they were provided with only a peck of corn a week. His overseer was ordered to procure coarse waled cloth enough to make each of them two garments a year. Hats and shoes were provided in winter for the wood-choppers and fence-builders, but for no others. The whole expense for food and clothing, reckoning the price of the corn and cloth at the market value, could not have exceeded ten dollars to each slave.

There was very little labor done on that plantation. One Northern man would perform as much as five of those slaves. And yet I never saw a more miserable, degraded, despairing family of human beings. Debts, taxes, and expenses of all kinds were paid by the sale of slaves, and the "soul driver" was an almost weekly visitor. There was not an unbroken family among them, — not even parents and children living together, excepting the mothers who were nursing their infants.

I frequently saw those mothers take their infants and their corn cake, at the sound of the horn at day break, and march in slow and solemn procession to the corn-fields. When they reached the place where they had left their hoes the evening before, a long distance from the huts, — as the fields near by had been worn out — they laid their infants down in the "gum cradles" — troughs cut in logs — and each one hoed a long row out and back in season to nourish the infants and eat the dinner-cake at noon. Then they hoed two more rows before returning to the cheerless huts, to rest their weary limbs at night. When they reached the huts, they took one quart of corn each, and putting it into a mortar — made by themselves by burning a hole into the end of a pine log — they pounded it into coarse meal with a wooden or iron pestle. After this they put one third of it into the kettle, and boiled it for supper, and then kneaded the remainder into a cake, and put it into the embers to be baked for breakfast and dinner the next day. They then laid down on the ground, — as the huts had no floors, — and slept, some on a few filthy old rags, others, on a thin layer of rice straw, until the horn called them again to perform their daily round of cheerless toil. One look at those slaves — and they had a kind master, if by kindness is only meant not to whip, or overtask — would have been sufficient to convince any Northern man that happiness is incompatible with such a condition.

When provisions are very scarce the slaves suffer much from hunger on some of the large plantations. "I have known slaves to suffer so much from hunger," said a gentleman to me residing in a place called 'Cave Run,' S. Carolina, "that they were accustomed to eat unclean beasts, and birds, fish, insects, and reptiles. I have known them to eat alligators, crows, owls, &c., and other things that nobody would eat if sufficient wholesome food could be obtained to keep them from starvation!"

"The dogs," he added, "fare better than the slaves, with some masters, — because whipping will not prevent the dog from stealing sheep, or fowls, when he is hungry."

"When I was a small boy," said a faithful slave belonging to J. R., of Cave Run, "I was set to cooking alligators for master's hounds, and an old slave woman frequently came to me to beg some of the cooked alligator to eat. She would say she was hungry — and I could not refuse her some dogs' meat."

"It was quite a large business," he continued, "to cook for thirty dogs; and it had to be done in style. I was often whipped for letting the dogs' dinner burn, or for letting them steal their food between meals — although I was not allowed to whip them — or for not having enough cooked ready for them when they would come home unexpectedly from a chase. And many a time have I wished I had been made a dog, instead of a slave, when I saw how much better the dogs fared than the slaves, and felt how much more kind their masters were to them than to me, and how much better they were treated in every respect than I was. It may seem strange to you, master, but *I envied the dog his condition!*"

I have heard much said about the time allowed to slaves to work for themselves, in cultivating gardens, and corn-patches, raising poultry &c. Those slaves who are indulged with such privileges are left, generally, to provide themselves with hats, and shoes, and tobacco, or any other little articles of luxury, — for which they must spend the avails of their labors on the Sabbath, or in the night, when they need to rest. But the number that are permitted to labor at all for such purposes is very small. Indeed I must say that very little regard is had to the comfort of the great mass of the slave population. There are many honorable *individual*, and a few *neighborhood* exceptions. But the great object of the master is to derive the greatest possible profit, at the least possible expense, provided that he does not endanger the life, and health, and value of his slaves. This is all that is comprehended in the pecuniary idea of slave labor.

In relation to the punishments to which slaves are exposed, and often subjected, it is not my purpose to give any detailed account. Occasional instances came under my notice, which I have narrated, in connection with other incidents. In this manner the reader may learn the facts quite as correctly, and much more agreeably to himself, than he could by perusing an entire chapter of sufferings and tortures. It is enough for any one who understands anything of human nature to know that the slave is helpless, powerless, unprotected, in the hands of his master. Admitting that slaveholders are no worse than other men, — it cannot be otherwise than true that their slaves often suffer terribly. The same number of Northern men, if they had the same power over their fellow creatures, if there were no restraints in society around them upon their passions — their anger, malice, revenge, cupidity, lust — would exhibit a degree of depravity of which we have now no conception.

I will, however, give a brief description of the instruments of torture which are in common use in the South. In this department the slaveholders exhibit more mechanical skill, and power of invention, than in their implements of husbandry.

THE THUMB SCREW.

I walked nine miles over bottom land, much of the way in water ankle deep, to see a slave who was wearing this instrument. The boy was riding a mule, in the cotton field, drawing a plow which was held by his mother. I inquired his age — but neither the mother nor son could give it. I judged him to be about sixteen. He had been wearing the screw two days. He said that it caused him but little pain at first; but after the swelling commenced in the thumb, the pain continued to increase, and he was already suffering so much that he said he would die before he would ever have it put on again.

The apparatus consists of a wristband of iron, with an iron stud or post about three inches long standing up in it opposite the thumb. A thin strap of iron passes around the ball of the thumb, attached to a piece of round iron, which runs back through a hole in the top of the post. Upon the end of this round iron is cut a screw, and behind the post a nut is put on. When this nut is turned, the thumb is drawn backward. The instrument is strong enough to dislocate the thumb by this retraction. The greatest amount of suffering which man is able to endure can be inflicted upon the slave with this instrument, and no scar remains to reduce his value in the market. By a long application the large nerves of the thumb become highly inflamed, and the most intense pain ensues.

The poor boy whom I saw wearing it, perished under the first application. The agony became so intense as to induce the lockjaw. As soon as it was known, the instrument was removed, and a physician employed; but his aid afforded no relief. Death came to release the suffering slave from the tyrant's power.

THE STOCKS.

Two pine planks, about two inches in thickness, one foot in width, and two feet in length, have each two semilunar notches cut in the edges, near the middle, just large enough to take in half of the ankle. One of these planks is applied to each side of the ankle, the edges of the planks are brought together, and then wooden cleats, running across the planks, are fastened on with wooden pins or iron spikes. The slaves are put in these stocks to prevent them from running away. They are so closely fitted to the ankle that the foot cannot be drawn out, made so strong that they cannot be broken, and so heavy that they cannot be dragged.

THE BELL.

The name does not indicate that this is an instrument of much suffering, — and yet the wearer finds it to be so. An iron belt passes around the loins — fastened over the spine with a lock, and a socket about half an inch in diameter. An iron collar is put around the neck, with an iron ring about an inch in diameter, fastened to the collar behind. A rod of round iron runs down through the ring at the back of the neck, and rests in the socket of the belt below. Above the neck this rod is split, and bent out in the shape of two horns, rising about a foot above the head. A cross-piece of iron is fastened to the top of the horns, and from the center of the cross-piece the "bell"— a common cow-bell — is suspended. The collar on the neck is often nearly as wide as the neck is long, and the upper edge sometimes is serrated — like a saw. Whenever the wearer turns his head, the collar chafes his neck. The bell is put on slaves that have been guilty of running away, so that they may be heard as they run, if they make another attempt. Besides, the apparatus is so heavy, and the horns so high and broad, that little progress can be made with it on, in the woods.

This instrument is not often applied, and I was obliged to travel fourteen miles to see one in use. The slave who wore it was driving a mule, in a cotton gin. Whenever Cuffee raised his hand to strike the mule, the bell would sound, and the animal was thus warned of the impending blow.

THE GAG.

The Gag is a piece of iron, about three inches in length, one inch in width at one end, half an inch at the other, and about one eighth of an inch in thickness. This instrument is put into the mouth, over the tongue, with the narrow end inside, while the wide end is left projecting through the lips. The outer end is inserted into a small strap of iron that passes over the mouth, the ends of which extend around to the back of the neck, where they are fastened together by a rivet, or a padlock. With this long, wide piece of iron thus confined on the tongue, the slave is truly gagged, — as he is unable to utter a syllable.

I saw the gag on a slave *preacher*, who, contrary to his orders, had left his hut in the night, and gone out into the woods to preach to some slaves, who had also left their huts without leave, to go and hear him. It was dangerous to allow such liberty to slaves. But

"Sambo" thought it his duty to preach in the night, even if he became a martyr by it, as there was much religious interest excited among the slaves by his preaching. He had been punished severely in various ways for his night preaching, — until his master's patience had been exhausted, and he told him that if he found him out again at midnight, he would shoot him. But death, if met in the path of duty, had no terrors for Sambo. When the appointed hour came, his flambeau blazed on the stump, and words of earnest Christian counsel and consolation were dropping from his lips, when Mr. B., his master, drew near to the devout worshippers, with his loaded rifle. With a stealthy step, he advanced slowly through the dark pine woods, until nearly within gun-shot of his victim, when the crackling of some dry limbs under his feet startled the outer guard, and the alarm ran through the listening crowd, reaching Sambo's ear. Mr. B. halted, and leaned against a tree, while waiting for the fears which his footsteps had created to pass away. Sambo continued to preach. The musical tones of his voice, the Christian heroism exhibited in his resignation to his fate, the moral courage displayed in recognizing his superior obligations to a higher power, the hearty responses which arose from his hearers, as he counseled obedience to their masters, and a patient endurance of sufferings for their Heavenly Master's sake, touched the heart of Mr. B., — who was himself a professor of the same faith — and changed his purpose. He decided to retire silently, and wait until morning before punishing the disobedient slave. In the morning Sambo was taken to the blacksmith to be gagged. After the rough iron had been thrust into his mouth, and fastened there, it was useless for him to run off in the night to preach again, for he could not speak a word. As I looked upon this preacher, thus compelled by his master to be *dumb*, I could not avoid the reflection that, after all, his condition was not unlike that of many of his Northern brethren,—though it doubtless causes less pain to be gagged with cotton, than with iron. It is but just to say, however, that since the passage of the Nebraska bill, the proportion of Northern ministers that are gagged by the Slave Power is far less than it was before.

COTTON PLANTER'S WHIP.

This is called the "Cotton planter's whip," because the planters say that *this whip raises the cotton.* The stock is covered with green hide, about four feet long, and is loaded with lead at the butt. The lash is long and heavily wrought into hard knots towards the end, with wire. The staff is so heavy, and the lash is so long, that the whipping-master is obliged to twirl it skilfully in the air before he can command its full force. Hence the labor of using this whip is hard, and when several hundred lashes are ordered, the whippers take turns.

THE PADDLE.

This is made of a board, and is about three feet long, and four inches wide. One end is shaved down for the handle, and the other end is bored full of half inch auger holes. The paddle is sometimes applied to the back of a slave until all the skin is taken off by it, so that no scar will remain to reduce the value of the slave in the market.

GANG CHAIN.

This is a long chain, running the whole length between the pairs of slaves marching in droves to the market. And the short chains between each pair are fastened to the long gang chain, and to a strong iron collar, fastened by a padlock around the neck of each slave.

There are other means resorted to for punishing slaves, which I need not describe. They are confined in the "sugar houses," — made to walk the "tread-mill," — and fastened together, or bound with "hand-cuffs." And aside from any regular instrument of torture, a master, or a mistress, or an overseer, in a fit of rage, will seize whatever weapon is at hand, and use it for this purpose. And the occasions, or the frequency of such inflictions depend on a thousand circumstances which cannot be foreseen, and which it would be useless for me to specify. I leave the subject, as one of the most unpleasant that came under my observation during my Southern tour.

XV.

FOOTPRINTS OF SLAVERY.

"Come! by whatever sacred name disguised,
Oppression, come! and in thy works rejoice!
See nature's richest plains to putrid fens
Turned by thy fury. From their cheerful bounds
See razed th' enlivening village, farm, and seat."

THOMPSON.

THE disastrous influence of slavery upon industrial pursuits, and its destructive effects upon the prosperity of communities, as well as of individuals, are seen in the South in every department of life, and among all classes of society. They are therefore incidentally traced in all the chapters of this narrative. But my object in this chapter is to group together some facts illustrating this truth more particularly, and exhibiting it in a stronger light.

All progress and all retrogression are perhaps relative, rather than absolute, and can best be shown by comparison or contrast. But if I indulge in this, my pictures may be colored, or at least some may suppose them to be, by my predilections for the North. I will, therefore, put into a frame of my own, — surrounding them with occasional views taken by myself during my various excursions, — some pencilings drawn by the slaveholders themselves. *They*, certainly, will not be accused of prejudice against the South. And I will first copy from a speech of Hon. W. C. Preston, of South Carolina, as reported in the *Columbia Telescope*. At the time of its delivery he had represented that State in the U. S. Senate for nearly six years, and he continued a member of that body for more than six years afterwards. But not more on account of his high position in the South, than of his power of graphic and life-like delineation, are his remarks worthy of our careful attention.

"No Southern man can journey,—as I have lately done,—through the Northern States, and witness the prosperity, the industry, the public spirit which they exhibit—the sedulous cultivation of all those arts by which life is rendered comfortable and respectable—without feelings of deep sadness and shame, as he remembers his own neglected and desolate home. There, no dwelling is to be seen abandoned, no farm uncultivated. Every person, and every thing, performs a part toward the grand result, and the whole land is covered with fertile fields, with manufactories, and canals, and railroads, and edifices, and towns, and cities. Along the route of the great New York canal (that glorious monument to the memory of De Witt Clinton), a canal, a railroad, and a turnpike are to be seen in the width of perhaps a hundred yards, each of them crowded with travel, or overflowing with commerce. Throughout their course, lands that before their construction would scarcely command five dollars the acre, now sell for fifty, seventy-five, or a hundred. Passing along it, you see no space of three miles without a town or village, and you are never out of the sound of a church bell.

"We of the South are mistaken in the character of these people, when we think of them only as peddlers in horn flints and bark nutmegs. Their energy and enterprise are directed to all objects, great and small, within their reach. At the fall of a scanty rivulet they set up their little manufactory of wooden buttons or combs — they plant a barren hill-side with broom corn, and make it into brooms at the bottom — and on its top they erect a wind-mill. Thus at a single spot you may see the air, the earth, and the water, all working for them. But at the same time the ocean is whitened to its extremities with the sails of their ships, and the land is covered with their works of art and usefulness.

"Massachusetts is perhaps one of the most flourishing of the Northern States. Yet of natural productions she exports but two articles — granite and ice. Absolutely nothing but *rock and ice!* Everything else of her commerce, from which she derives so much, is artificial — the work of her own hands.

"All this is done, in a region with a bleak climate and sterile soil, by the energy and intelligence of the people. Every man knows that the public good is his individual advantage. The number of railroads and other modes of expeditious intercommunication, knits the whole country into a closely compacted mass, through which the productions of commerce and of the press, the comforts of life and the means of knowledge, are universally diffused; while the close intercourse of travel and business makes all neighbors, and promotes a common interest and a common sympathy.

"In a community thus connected, a single flash of thought pervades the whole land, almost as rapidly as thought itself can fly. The population becomes, as it were, a single set of muscles, animated by one heart, and directed by a common sensorium.

"How different the condition of these things in the South! Here, the face of the country wears the aspect of premature old age and decay. No improvement is seen going on — nothing is done for posterity — no man thinks of any thing beyond the present moment. Our lands are yearly tasked to their utmost capacity of production, and when exhausted, are abandoned for the youthful West. Because nature has been prodigal to us, we seem to think it unnecessary to do any thing for ourselves. The industry and skill that have converted the inclement and barren hills of New England into a garden, of the climate and fertile soil of the South would create almost a paradise. Our natural advantages are among the greatest with which Providence has blessed mankind, but we lack the spirit to improve and enjoy them. The rich ore is beneath our feet, yet we dig not for it. The golden fruit hangs from the bough, and we lift not our hands to gather it. The cask of delicious liquor is before our eyes, but we are too lazy even to broach it."

It is true that Senator Preston does not attribute the striking contrast between the North and the South, which he thus so skillfully pictures, to the existence of slavery in the latter. Nor will I make any such assertion,—but will rather leave it for every one to come to whatever conclusion the facts will warrant. But for this purpose I will ask the reader's attention to a comparison of individual States, drawn partly from my own observation, and partly from the census report of 1850.

There are no two States in the Union so nearly equal in natural resources as Kentucky and Ohio,—though if there is any difference, it is in favor of the former. Kentucky has about the same area, and a somewhat milder climate than the northern part of Ohio,—but both States have a very fertile soil. Kentucky was settled first, and in 1790 had a population of 60,000, while Ohio was still a wilderness. In 1815 the latter had overtaken the former in population, and far surpassed it in wealth. In 1850 the population of Kentucky was 982,405, while that of Ohio was 1,980,427! Both are agricultural States, and raise very nearly the same kinds of produce—no rice or cotton of any consequence being cultivated in either. And though Kentucky had a million and a half acres of *improved* lands more than Ohio, the value of farm lands in the former was $ 154,330,262,—in the latter it was $ 358,758,603! The value of farming implements and machinery in the first was $ 5,169,037,—in the last, $ 12,750,585! If this astonishing difference in the prosperity and growth of these two States, during the last fifty years, is not explained by the fact that one is a slave State, and the other free, how can we explain it? What other cause can be assigned?

As it is the turn of the South to give us the next picture, I will quote from a pamphlet published in 1840 by Hon. Thomas F. Marshal, a distinguished politician of Kentucky.

"In 1790, Virginia, with 70,000 square miles of territory, contained a population of 749,308. New York, upon a surface of 46,000 square miles, contained a population of 344,120. This statement exhibits in favor of Virginia a difference of 24,000 square miles of territory, and 408,108 in population,—which is double that of New York and 68,000 more. In 1830, after a race of forty years, Virginia is found to contain 1,211,405 souls, and New York 1,918,608. Virginia has increased in the ratio of 61 per cent, and New York in that of 566 per cent!" [In 1850 the population of Virginia was 1,421,661, or less than double that of 1790, while that of New York was 3,097,394, being *nine times* its population in 1790! The value of farming lands in Virginia in 1850 was $216,401,441. In New York it was $554,546,642!]

Mr. Marshal continues:—"Statesmen may differ about policy, or the means to be employed in the promotion of the public good; but surely they ought to be agreed as to what prosperity means. I think there can be no dispute that New York is a greater, richer, and more prosperous State than Virginia. What has occasioned the difference? There is but one explanation of the facts I have shown. The clog that has staid the march of her people, the incubus that has weighed down her enterprise, strangled her commerce, kept sealed her exhaustless fountains of mineral wealth, and paralyzed her arts, manufactures, and improvements, is negro slavery."

In confirmation of this conclusion, I noticed wherever I traveled in the South that the old counties, which were first settled, were uniformly inferior to the new counties in population and wealth. I do not include in this statement those counties which contain large cities on the seaboard, as other causes contribute to their prosperity. But wherever the influence of slavery has been felt the longest, the soil is the most barren, the buildings the poorest or the most dilapidated, the schools and churches the fewest, and the people the most ignorant and degraded.

Virginia is the oldest of the States. In her productions, her harbors, and rivers, she is unequaled in her advantages for commerce, — foreign as well as domestic. But her trade is small, and is mostly carried on through the ports and the shipping of the North. No Northern State has equal natural advantages for manufactures, and yet they are almost entirely unimproved. The value of her cotton manufactures in 1850 was only $ 1,486,384, — being a little more than half as much as those of Maine, and less than one twelfth as much as Massachusetts.

One of the most beautiful cities in this country is Richmond, the capital of Virginia; and it might have been one of the largest. Situated at the head of tide water on James River, it has a fine harbor, and is admirably located for commerce. The foreign arrivals in 1852 were 35, and the clearances for foreign ports 71.

The foreign clearances from Boston the same year were 2866, and the arrivals 2974. Richmond, like ancient Rome, is built on several hills. The scenery of its environs is unsurpassed for beauty and variety. Nor are its advantages limited to the beautiful. The river here descends about 100 feet, constituting one of the best waterpowers in the country. This, however, is but partially improved. There are some flouring mills, and a few tobacco factories. With a proper degree of enterprise, it would become one of the largest manufacturing cities in the Union. But it lies weak and powerless in the hands of slavery. In 1800 its population was 5,737, and that of Cincinnati was 750. Now, after a growth of fifty years, the population of Cincinnati is 160,000 — while that of Richmond is only 30,000, — of whom 10,000 are colored!

The State of Georgia contains very nearly as much territory as the whole of New England, and is divided into ninety-seven counties. In this State I could see more distinctly than in any other the effects of slavery on the soil and the population. There are six counties on the sea coast, — the earliest settled in the State, and the most fertile. If we except the city of Savannah, whose prosperity depends on the interior, the whole number of whites in the six counties is less than ten thousand. There are also six counties bordering on the northern line of the State, some three hundred miles in the interior, all of them *new*, — and yet they contain a free population of forty-five thousand. A comparison of the six counties next in order, in each section of the

State, shows the same result. The *new* counties, far back from the seaboard, contain forty-seven thousand whites, while the *old* counties, though large in territory, contain only fourteen thousand.

The city of Darien also furnishes an illustration of the same truth. It is one of the oldest cities in Georgia, having been settled by some Scotch Highlanders in 1736. It was once in a flourishing condition, and before the lands in the lower counties had been exhausted, it had an extensive trade in produce. But the country around it has become sterile and barren, and the trade of the northern part of the State has been diverted to Savannah and Charleston by the construction of railroads. The result is that Darien has become like an old, deserted castle, dilapidated and decayed. Though a port of entry, its whole shipping in 1852 was 306 tons registered, and 859 enrolled. And during the same year its foreign arrivals were only three!

Under a free labor system this would have been a large and prosperous city. It is situated at the mouth of the Altamaha river, which, with its tributaries, the Oconee and the Ocmulgee, furnishes more than three hundred miles of inland navigation, through a country all of it once, and much of it still fertile, abounding in extensive forests of oak and pine. That an old city, surrounded with such advantages, should be reduced to a pitiable village, with only 550 inhabitants, is a problem that nothing but slavery can solve!

The city of Charleston, S. C., exhibits another illustration, of a different kind, though not less striking.

There are few cities that surpass this in beauty; and it has extensive advantages for business. Connected by railroad with the principal towns in North Carolina, the northern part of Georgia, and Tennessee, it has some permanent sources of prosperity. It exports more rice than any other city in the Union, and more cotton than any other except New Orleans and Mobile.

But though Charleston has been increasing, the large county of the same name, of which it is the center, containing 1900 square miles, once one of the most fertile and productive in the State, is decreasing in population. In 1840 it was 82, 000, and 1850 only 72,000, though the city during that time increased from 29,000 to 42,000. Thus it is seen that this county, exclusive of the city, contained in 1840 a population of 53,000, and in 1850 only 30,000. A decrease of 23,000 in ten years! Such has always been the history of slave countries. Their temporary prosperity, sometimes dazzling and brilliant, is but a prelude to approaching decay and ruin. It soon

> "Touches the highest point of all its greatness,
> And from the full meridian of its glory,
> It hastens to its setting."

XVI.

NO SYMPATHY FOR SLAVES.

> "Thou art come to answer
> A stony adversary, an inhuman wretch,
> Incapable of pity, void and empty
> From every drachm of mercy." SHAKESPEARE.

THE slaveholders manifest little regard for the happiness of the slaves. It may not be evident to them all, but still it is true, that the family training, the intellectual discipline, the circulating intelligence of the slave States, are not such as to open in the heart and mind of the master a single well-spring of generous sympathy for them, — even in times of bereavement, of deepest sorrow, or when suffering the anguish of severe punishment, or even when in the agonies of death, in its most terrible forms! This is not always apparent, except where none but slaveholders are present to witness the death-struggle of their victims, — or where the slave is made to suffer publicly, as a warning to others.

I left the hotel in M. after breakfast on a December morning, and walked a few miles along the bank of the Flint river. Ascending a small sand hill, I saw, after reaching the top, a negro coming up on the other side, slowly, wearily, without a particle of clothing on. When he saw me, he was frightened and ran out to a willow tree that lay bent down, nearly horizontally, over the stream; and turning about, he leaned against a limb, looking at me, and tossing up his hands, he exclaimed, imploringly, "O, Goddy, master!"

I supposed he intended to request me not to betray him; and I said to him, "I will not betray you, Cuffee!" But before I had time to inquire into his history, two hounds came over another hill, half a mile distant, distinctly in view, on a straight road. Soon as the baying of the dogs reached the ear of the fugitive, he leaped from the willow into the river — swam a long distance under water towards the opposite bank, when he arose to the surface. I was surprised to see how directly he swam across, as the waters were cold, and the current strong. I saw him emerge upon the opposite side, climb an oak tree, and seat himself on a limb. The hounds came on slowly, following the track, — and well they might, for the blood of the slave was left in nearly every footstep — keeping up a constant baying. I had heard of "the baying of hounds," but I had never conceived how appalling the blood-thirsty tones were, until they fell on my ear, while I saw their victim, weary and helpless, with no longer any hope of escape.

The dogs came up the hill where I stood, followed the track out upon the willow, plunged in where the man did, swam across, and ran up to the tree, baying loudly in the triumph of success. I walked out to the willow and sat down upon it in sadness of heart at what my eyes had seen, and my ears heard. Soon two white men came over the farther hill on horse back, and when they saw the man in the tree, and heard the dogs baying beneath it, they set up a tremendous shout, and rode on at full speed down to the tavern, three miles below. Thinking it might be unsafe for me to remain and watch the fate of the slave, whom I had no power to assist, I returned to the tavern. Here I found a large crowd of men who had gathered around the bar to receive a "*treat*" from the "nigger hunters," who always have that kind of glorification when the man is captured alive. It was now about nine o'clock, yet they continued to drink until four o'clock in the afternoon, before they went over the river to take the man down.

And what astonished me more than any thing else, was, that no man suggested that it was time to go and bring the slave in. I heard no question asked as to how long he had been without food, how far he had run, or whether he was so famished and exhausted that he would be likely to fall from the tree and be rent in pieces by the dogs. But the conversation ran mainly upon the feats they had performed in the negro hunts, and the punishments the runaways get when they are caught. Finally, after seven hours of rioting, they rode away. What became of their poor victim I never learned.

The hound is taught to regard the slave as his natural enemy. The slave is never allowed to chastize him. If the dog is stealing his dinner, he may push him away gently, or pull his dinner away from him, — but he must not venture to pull his ears, or scold him, or strike him, on pain of being whipped himself by his master.

I saw a slaveholder near M. teaching puppies to hunt slaves. He was the owner of a slave mother and her little boy, Harry, who was about four years old. The mother was a *light quadroon,* having just enough of African blood to wave the long black hair, and gloss the full, black eye. There are large numbers of such slave girls in the South, and a foreigner has truly said that they are the most beautiful specimens of American women. But her little Harry was not so light colored, and he had rough, hard, features. He was a very sensible boy, roguish and reckless, and he acted as though the bad blood of all his ancestors ran in his veins. His "bump of destructiveness" was very large, and it very often cost him a flogging. He killed all the kittens about house, all the chickens he could catch, broke all the eggs he could find, destroyed all the crockery he could lay hold of, and left his mark on every piece of furniture in the house, and on every tool and carriage on the premises.

He had a peculiar dislike to turkies. No turkey could be raised, except in a yard with a fence so high that Harry could not climb it. A close, high fence was made around the turkey yard, and they were regarded as secure from the enemy. But Harry ran a little pole up to the top of the fence, climbed up, jumped in, and killed thirteen turkies — a mother and twelve little ones. In his haste to kill the turkies, he forgot to run the pole over on the inside, so that he could get out; and being obliged to call for help, the "murder was out." Sambo opened the door to release him, and seeing the turkies killed, he ran into the house and told his master. Harry had been indulged quite enough by his master, as he was an idol, only son of his mother, "Hatty." And she was the favorite slave of her master, Col. V., who had uniformly regarded the feelings of the tender-hearted, doting mother so far as not to punish Harry in her presence. But this provocation threw him into a passion.

"Hatty!" exclaimed the master, "go and bring the little devil to me."

Hatty went out and led in Harry, who appeared quite self-possessed, and without fear of punishment. But his mother saw that her master was enraged, and imagining some terrible thing was contemplated in the use of the knife, which Col. V. held in one hand, while he reached out the other and exclaimed passionately, "hand him to me! I'll fix him!" she ventured to say — "don't master! don't cut him with the knife!"

"Hold your tongue!" said the master, "and set the boy on my knee, and hold him still!"

Grasping one ankle with the left hand, he commenced cuting small gashes through the skin on the bottom of the foot. Harry strove like a hero, kicked and squirmed; struck his master in the face, and pulled his hair; but he succeeded in cutting both feet till the blood ran freely!

Col. V. then told his son to lead Harry out around the stable, by a circuitous route, to a low, pine tree, to which he pointed, about twenty rods distant. Hatty was ordered to cut up a plate of raw beef in small pieces, and bring it to him.

The Col. took the plate of meat in his hand, went to the kennel and unchained the mother of seven blood-hound puppies, and led her around on the track of Harry, with the puppies following after. At every few steps he dropped a piece of the meat, on the blood which was left in Harry's track, for the puppies to eat, where they would receive the scent of the blood of the slave! When he arrived at the tree, he sent his son back with the mother of the puppies, while they remained to eat the meat given to them under the tree. Harry was taken down from the limb on which he sat, and the little hounds were taught to bite his feet, around which pieces of meat were thrown. Hatty, in the meantime, was wringing her hands as if her heart were bursting, and as though she had forgotten that she was a favorite house servant, and had a kind, indulgent master.

One day while I was in the city of M., there was a terrible outcry in the streets!

"What 's the matter?"

"A negro in the creek!"

"Where?"

"Out over the railroad bridge."

And all the city rushed into the street, and over the bridge. I followed on with the crowd. Besides the negro, two hounds were in the creek also, endeavoring to catch him. He would dive and swim a long distance under water, so deep that the dogs could not see the direction he took; but when he raised his head above water to breathe, the dogs swam towards him and seized his limbs and held on till he jerked them away, leaving his flesh in their teeth. Soon his pursuers were seen coming from the woods, and he perceived that farther attempts to elude them were vain, and he came out of the creek and gave himself up to the hunters. Two of them dismounted, and took him, one by either arm, to lead him over the bridge into the city, in the midst of the vast, exulting multitude.

A friend of mine, an intelligent New England merchant, was present. He expressed to me his astonishment that no sympathy was manifested for the suffering slave, whose bare limbs were horridly lacerated by the dogs. And what most shocked his feelings, as the men were leading him, was to hear the boys tell the dogs to bite him — saying, "seek him! take him!"— just as they would set dogs on swine in the street, and with as little pity.

The negro pretended to be so weak that he could hardly walk; but when about on the center of the bridge, he prostrated one of the men who were holding his arms — broke away from the grasp of the other — rushed through the crowd — bounded over the railing, and sank in the red waters of the river, to rise no more. No word of pity was heard, — no emotions of sympathy were witnessed, for the sufferings and fate of this man, who had less fear of death than of *his brother man!*

But the air was filled with curses on "runaway niggers," and a grand chorus of invectives against abolitionists concluded the awful tragedy!

A WHITE MOTHER FOR SALE.

Mr. C., a dry goods merchant of Boston, was with me at the little city of M., where he went to visit a partner in trade. He had not been in a slave State before, and was bitterly opposed to emancipation. Two merchants — slaveholders — had been in our company on the way to that city. Whenever slavery was talked of, Mr. C. uniformly concurred with them. The next morning after we arrived, we saw a handbill in the bar-room in which forty-four female slaves were advertised for sale. Stepping out into the street, we found those girls sitting on the sidewalks. At the farther end of the row was a very beautiful girl, apparently perfectly white, and neatly dressed. The moment Mr. C. looked at her, he exclaimed, "What do you think that white girl is sitting there with those negroes for?"

"I presume she is a slave, sir," said I.

"That can't be!" replied Mr. C.,—"just look at her! Why I never saw a prettier girl in my life."

Now Mr. C. had heard that *likely quadroons* are held as slaves and sold in the market; but he had never believed that a young *lady*, so entirely American, so elegant in form and feature, so intellectual in appearance, with pure blue eyes, and the perfect red and white Caucassian complexion, was in the same degraded condition as the African girl. And his fine sensibilities were greatly shocked at the idea, that a white girl, so beautiful, was doomed to such disgrace. His heart was steeled against sympathy for the blacks, but it was unshielded on the side towards the white race, to which his mother, wife, and daughter belonged. Hence he was unprepared to believe it, when I said to him, "*she is a slave, sir!*"

There was the precise number, including her, advertised in the bill. Still incredulous, Mr. C. stepped up to the drover and asked, "Is that white girl a slave, sir?"

"That 's not a white girl; she is a nigger, sir," replied the drover.

Mr. C. bit his lips with suppressed indignation, paused, and then ejaculated, "Is it possible!"

"Does she belong to *you?*" said he to the drover.

"Yes, sir!" replied the drover.

"What do you ask for her?" inquired Mr. C.

"I was offered 1800 dollars for her last night. I want 2000 for her."

"What do you ask for that one?" said Mr. C., pointing to a light quadroon sitting next to the white girl.

"I will take $1,200 for her."

"Well,—how much for the black ones, here at this end of the row?"

"I will take $800 apiece," replied the slave-dealer.

"Why can that white girl—

"That isn't a white girl; that 's a *nigger*, sir, I tell you," interrupted the drover, contemptuously. At the same time he removed a woolen cap from her head, which exposed the light brown hair, and added, "you see her hair is waved."

This is regarded as evidence that African blood is mingled with the white. Mr. C. had now become excited, and he exclaimed — "Well, then, can that *white nigger* do more work than one of your *black* niggers, that you ask so much more for her?"

"Oh no;" replied the drover, — and perceiving that Mr. C. did not comprehend the superior value of female beauty to physical ability in a slave, he added — "but you know she is a high priced *fancy* girl."

"By heavens!" vociferated Mr. C., "'tis too bad!" and turning to me with his clinched hands raised towards the heavens, he added, "I will never say another word against the abolitionists, so long as God lets me live!"

We inquired of those mothers, how many children they had left behind; and the aggregate number — as by them reported — was *one hundred and twenty-four!* They were all enrolled as being between the ages of eighteen and twenty-five, in the advertising catalogue. Forty-four young mothers severed from their husbands and all their children at a single blow!!!

I became acquainted with a good slave boy, "Bill," owned by A. S., in South Carolina. He was a cruel master, worked his slaves very hard, and gave them only a peck of corn a week. I asked Bill if he ever knew a slave to get a whipping when he did not deserve it.

"Well, master," replied Bill, "I will tell you the cause for which I had a terrible whipping, and I will let you decide whether it was deserved. Our driver's name was Monday, — a colored man. One day I heard Monday say that if master S. did not treat him better, he meant to run away. Now I loved Uncle Monday, — as we called him — and I ran up to him and said, thoughtlessly, — without any more intention of running away than I had of killing myself — 'if you run away, I mean to run away too!'

"The master was listening outside the hut — as slaveholders often are, to hear what is said by the slaves — and he heard me. He rushed into the hut in a terrible passion, caught me by the throat, kicked me, and threw me down, and beat me, — crying out at intervals, with terrific oaths — 'You want to run away, do you! I'll give you enough of running away! I'll learn Old Monday better than to spoil all my young niggers!'

"After he had beaten me awhile in the hut, he dragged me out, and called a large man to come and help tie me up to a timber that projected from the eaves of the house. He then tied my feet together, and thrusting a rail between them to keep me from swinging, he climbed up, and with a rope fastened to my wrists, he drew me up until my feet were raised from the earth. Every particle of my ragged garments had been stripped from my body, — and he ordered one of the house girls to bring him the whip. When the girl came with it, he told her to go back and bring a quart of salt. The salt was brought, and he dissolved it in water. Then he took off his coat, rolled up his sleeves, and seized the whip — the staff of which was four or five feet long, made of white oak, covered with raw hide, the butt about two inches thick, loaded with lead, and the lash at least six feet long, with several inches of the end wrought into hard knots with catgut. With this instrument I was whipped until the master became tired, when he commanded the slave to continue to flog me until I had received one hundred lashes. Several times during this flogging I fainted away. The whipping was suspended, and cold water thrown upon me until I recovered, when it was resumed. I should judge they were whipping me nearly an hour. The salt and water was then thrown upon me, and coals of fire would not have given me more unutterable torment."

I became acquainted with another slave boy called "Jack," in the State of S. Carolina, who was highly spoken of by every one that knew him. Jack's master, J. R., was always kind when sober — but never when intoxicated. One day he whipped Jack severely for running away.

"In a few days after this whipping," said Jack, as he was giving me a short history of his life, "I told a slave, in confidence, that I meant to run away again. He betrayed me, and informed Master of my purpose. This greatly enraged him, and he sent for a neighboring planter and his overseer to come and whip me. The first intimation I had of it, the overseer rushed into the hut, and struck me over the face with the but of his whip, cutting my cheek through to the bone, — and the scar is still a witness to the deed. Then they tied me, and carried me into the yard, and my master and the overseer both whipped me at the same time.

"When slaves are whipped, they usually make a great ado, for the purpose of mitigating the punishment. If they cry out piteously, saying '*do, pray* Massa, forgive me, I'll do work better,' &c., — they usually get a less number of lashes. So at this time I said every thing I could think of. When I cried loud for forgiveness, they would tauntingly reply — 'you've learned to halloo at the night meetings, have you?'— meaning religious meetings. And they crammed old rags into my mouth, so that I could not be heard across the street.

"After the whipping was finished, the flaying paddle was applied, and I was then taken to the barn-yard and chained to the sill of the barn, having the chain locked around my neck. They raked up some corn husks for me to lie on, but my back and sides were so sore I could not lie down, but was obliged to lean against the barn, in which miserable position I passed the long, dreary, suffering, sleepless night! In the morning I was tied upon a horse, and driven four miles, to be ironed. The blacksmith took some old ox shoes and beat them together, in the shape of two half moons, and riveted them at the corners, so as to fit the ankle, stood me upon the anvil, and fastened them on. I was then set to hoeing cotton again, and ten rows were added to my daily task."

XVII.

SOUTHERN JURISPRUDENCE.

"It well becomes the judge to nod at crimes,
That does commit greater himself."

TOURNEUR.

"Do not your juries give their verdict,
As if they felt the cause, — not heard it?
And as they please, make every fact
Run all one side, — as they are packed?"

BUTLER.

THAT there are able lawyers in the South, no one will deny. There are also some eminent judges, whose legal learning and sense of justice go hand in hand. In this respect, however, there is a difference in the Southern States. The northern slave States have a better system of jurisprudence than the southern, — if we except Louisiana, which stands far better than Mississippi, Alabama, and Georgia. But aside from any individual exceptions, the administration of justice throughout the South is far more imperfect and partial than it is in the North. The slaveholders are an aristocracy, holding the offices, enacting the laws, and, as judges or sheriffs, controlling their execution. And so much does the spirit of *caste* enter into all the institutions of the slave States, that favoritism is often a predominant principle, even within the temples of justice. The trial and acquittal of Ward in Kentucky is a prominent illustration; and no one can spend much time in the South without observing numerous incidents of a like character.

A Southern writer has recently boasted that there is less crime in the South than in the North, — appealing to the number of convictions and imprisonments reported, as evidence of it. But no such inference can be drawn from this fact — as I shall abundantly show. Prisons in the South are indeed few and poor, compared with those of the North, and the inmates less in number; but this is not because crime is not more frequent, but because it goes unpunished.

The crimes of slaves are not often made a matter of trial and punishment in the Southern courts. The master is the judge, the jury, and the executioner. That the slaves are often guilty of crimes is just what we might expect. Aside from the vicious examples of unbridled passion and indulgence which are constantly before them, and of which they are often the victims, — their ignorance and degradation, the smothering of all the better feelings in their natures, the extinguishing of all those hopes and aspirations which tend to elevate and purify the heart, while the baser elements are left free and unchecked, and often strengthened by the wrongs they suffer, all contribute to brutalize and degrade them. And when I have learned of their committing revolting crimes, instead of being surprised, I have wondered that the instances are not far more frequent.

The ceaseless, unremitting toil of the slaves undoubtedly tends to save them from the commission of crime. While, on the other hand, the idleness and consequent dissipation of the slaveholding class are the source of that fearful catalogue of offences of which we sometimes catch a glimpse. And lest I might seem to exaggerate in the incidents which I relate, I will call the reader's attention to an extract from a recent lecture of Rev. James A. Lyon, pastor of the Presbyterian church in Columbus, Mississippi, published in the *Eagle*, a newspaper of that city, June 1st, 1855.

"The reckless manner in which the sixth commandment, which forbids murder, is disregarded in this community, is truly alarming, and should excite the well grounded fears of every friend of morality and good order. As proof that I am not exaggerating the evil, I will refer you to the statistical tables on this subject for the last year, [1854.] In the Daily *Globe* for January 2d, 1855, quoted by the New York *Herald*, the following startling facts are brought to light, viz: That there have been in the United States, during the last year, no less than *six hundred and eighty-two* murders! and only eighty-four executions; that is, about *one in seven only!* Here is a little army slain every year, by the hands of violence, in our country, boasting justly of more *general* intelligence, freedom, and civilization than any other upon the globe! But let us examine a little this table of blood. We find that, of the murdered host, only *thirty-two* fell in the six New England States, only *one hundred and six* others in the Middle States, including the largest States and cities in the Union. The blood of all the rest, *five hundred and forty-four*, was spilt in the South and West. But let us inspect still more closely this record of crime. Of this remaining army, *five hundred and forty-four* strong, that have fallen in the South and West, *three hundred and forty-six* have been slaughtered in the *South* alone; that is, in the Southern States proper, not including Missouri, there have fallen more than one half of the whole of the original army! The South has the unenviable distinction of having slain a greater number of their fellow men with murderous hands than all the other States, including even California, put together! Of this number, I am sorry to say that as many as *thirty-two* have been slaughtered in our own proud State of Mississippi;* that is, in the State of Mississippi alone, as many human beings have fallen by the hand of violence, as in all the six New England States put together — States with an aggregate population five times as great as that of Mississippi! If the New England States had slain as many of their fellow men in proportion to their population as the State of Mississippi has done, instead of murdering only *thirty-two*, they would have murdered five times that number!

"We have no great seaport towns as the places of resort for felons of other lands; we have no foreign population amongst us, except such as belong to the

* The editor of the *Eagle* here says, in a note, that he a few years ago heard Gov. H. S. Foote say that some person had been killed within the State every day during his term of office of two years!

better classes of society; we are not a new and pioneer State; and yet the annual list of our murdered is *frightful!*—frightful not only on account of the comparative number of the slain, but also on account of the *character* and *standing* of the slayers. If these murders were committed by vagabonds and the scum of society, then its *prestige*, its moral effect, would not be so injurious to society. But what, think you, is the effect upon the minds of our children and youth, when men of fair standing in society, received and regarded as gentlemen, are the perpetrators of the butcheries!!

"In view of this state of things, who is safe? My enemy meets me, insults me, and then shoots me down, professing to believe that I was '*armed*,' as a matter of course, and that his *life* was in danger; tells his own story in a community where it is no strange thing for men to carry about their persons deadly weapons. Each one feels that he would have done the same thing under similar circumstances, so that in condemning him they would but condemn themselves. Consequently, the slayer is justified—goes free; and a hundred others, our sons and half grown lads amongst them, resolve in their hearts, that since every man may go armed, and every one is therefore justifiable in slaying his enemy, they will do likewise.

"I should like to deprecate the influence of money in setting aside the law. It is a shameful fact that *no rich man can be hanged for murder in the Southwest!* The man, therefore, who is able to pay a few thousand dollars, may indulge his dire revenge with impunity.

The frequency with which *slaves* are killed, and the little attention paid to it by the officers of the law, is a crying evil, which I had intended to dwell upon as its importance deserves."

In commenting upon this lecture, the editor of the *Eagle* says that

"The frequency of the open and violent murders committed in the South and Southwest, and especially within our own State, is the most remarkable, and at the same time the most disgraceful, characteristic of our section of the country. And it is equally strange and astonishing to us, that, instead of diminishing, as the tone of our society improves and the standard of civilization advances, this horrid and unnatural offence against humanity, good order, law, and morals, seems to be on the increase.

"The pulpit having led the way in the reform so loudly called for in regard to this matter, and called upon the press to follow in the noble and praiseworthy enterprise, we, for one, hesitate not a moment, but at once raise our voice and nerve our arm for the conflict against the hideous crime of murder, the almost daily commission of which, in some part of our State, is brought to our knowledge by, and as regularly as, our exchanges are received."

The fact stated by Mr. Lyon,—"that no rich man can be hanged for murder in the Southwest"—may appear strange; but the manner of organizing a court in the Southern States is almost sure to give impunity to offenders. Juries, in such cases, are empanneled from the crowd of bystanders, instead of being selected beforehand by the municipal authorities, as they are in the North. How easy for a wealthy slaveholder to have a score of dependents, from among his poor neighbors, standing around the court-room, where the Judge or the clerk will be likely to call them! This, more than any thing else, makes the administration of justice in the criminal courts of the South a mere farce.

I was in Baker county when Dr. Byrd, of Albany, killed a man by the name of Jones. Sometimes, when a free white man has become obnoxious to a neighborhood by constantly provoking quarrels and going about to do evil, priding himself on being a fighter, the slaveholders will be glad of an opportunity to arraign him, and either punish him or drive him off. Such a man was Dr. Byrd. He and Jones had a falling out, and Byrd demanded of Jones a card in the Albany Patriot, acknowledging that he had slandered him. Jones took the paper in which the card was published, and went to the tavern where Byrd boarded, and showed him the card. Byrd called for brandy,—a custom after such affairs are amicably adjusted. While sipping the liquor—as the landlord assured me—Jones patted Byrd on the shoulder and remarked, facetiously,

"The biggest lie I ever told in my life, Byrd, was when I said here in this card that I lied about you; for you know every word that I had said was true."

"You are a liar and a villain!" said Byrd, seizing his pistol.

Jones drew his knife, and cut Byrd severely in several

places. But Byrd shot him through the heart. He made one bound from the bar-room into the street, and expired.

Byrd was arrested and taken to Newton jail. It was reported in the papers that he had poisoned himself in the jail. But instead of that, he returned to Albany the next day, and in a short time he was established in the practice of his profession in Alabama.

Having business with R. K. Hines, Esq., a popular lawyer in the city of Albany, I inquired of him, after Byrd was carried to the jail, if he would be hung.

"Hung! my dear sir?" said Mr. H. "We have more cases on the docket in this county now, for murder, than can be tried during the next ten years. So that all Byrd's lawyer would have to do, in order to postpone a trial, would be to call up former cases before this."

"Is that possible, Mr. Hines?" said I.

"Why, let me tell you," replied Mr. H., "while we were trying a man for murder at the last court at Starkville, the next county seat above, two murders were committed within gun-shot of that court house."

Soon after this, I was in the stage, passing through Starkville. A young man stepped out of the coach when it stopped.

"That was John Ross," remarked a passenger, as the coach wheeled around to start again.

"Yes," said another, "John Ross that killed his father here!"

"And was never complained of!" responded a third.

"John Ross," said Col. L., "wanted to marry one of

his father's negro girls." And he proceeded to relate the facts as they had occurred.

John was an only child of a rich slaveholder. His father was bitterly opposed to this freak of his son, and he told him that he would not consent to have the blood corrupted in this manner. But John replied that he loved the black girl, and intended to marry her.

Now John was not peculiar in this fancy. Slaveholders very frequently marry the quadroon girls,— and some of them select the full-blooded Africans for their wives. Mr. A., the city surveyor in D., lost a white wife, and he then emancipated his black female cook, and married her. So that John Ross was not the first white man who had desired such a connubial relation. But his father was invincibly opposed to his wishes; and he informed his son that if he persisted in his foolish purpose to marry that "nigger," he would disown and disinherit him. And when all arguments had failed, and John finally assured the old gentleman that his purpose was fixed to marry that girl, the father banished him from his house.

John took lodgings in a public house, near by. His mother had been dead several years, and now the father sat solitary and alone, without an heir. He had great possessions, and he knew he must shortly leave them. And to whom? "*Poor John! Foolish son!*" he said to himself. "I will call him home, and make one more attempt to bring him back to regard the honor of the family, for his blessed mother's sake." And the father sent his son a note, stating that he desired to have an interview with him, that he might, if possible, dissuade him from his rrsh purpose; but at all events to have a reconciliation.

"John Ross," said Col. L., "loaded his rifle, put in that kind letter, received from his father, for wadding, and the first time the father stepped over the threshold of his own door, he was shot dead by that unnatural son!"

John was a chivalrous, "*dead shot*" Southron. Nobody dared enter a complaint against him for the murder of his father. Besides, young John, — now made sole proprietor of a large estate by this heroic deed, — gave valuable presents to the slaveholding neighbors, and public opinion made no other or higher demand.

Throughout the slave States, a light value is set upon human life. The murderer has no fear of punishment, if he has wealth and rank to protect him. Slaveholders risk their lives on the most fantastic whim of honor. We know it to be a false notion of honor, but the Southron regards it as the highest ambition of his life to maintain it. Hence the cold blooded, fatal rencounters so frequent in the South. This is illustrated by the following facts, which were stated in my presence by Col. L. of Alabama.

"I was sitting at a dinner table in Texas," said Col. L., "when two young gentlemen came in from a hunting excursion. They walked up to the sideboard, took a glass of whisky, and then seated themselves at the table. A. sat next to me, and B. directly opposite to him. A. called for some meat, but B. sat mute. I noticed there was a malicious, designing, murderous look in his countenance, and I suspected that there was trouble near. In a few moments A. said to B.,

"I now ask you, sir, in the presence of these gentlemen, if you will publicly retract the malicious slanders you have put in circulation, seriously affecting my reputation as an honorable man and a gentleman?"

"No!" said B. "You are a dishonest villain, and I will never perjure myself to save your reputation!"

A. drew out a brace of pistols, threw them down on the table, and exclaimed,

"Take your choice of them, sir!"

B. arose, took a white handkerchief from his pocket, wound one corner of it around the little finger of his left hand, tossed the other end to his antagonist, who rose up, wound that end around the little finger of his hand, like the other, bringing their left hands within six inches of each other. Then each took a pistol in the right hand, pointed it directly at the other's heart, and at the word '*ready*' they commenced to count the usual number in such cases. Both counted, slowly, distinctly, simultaneously, 'one—two—three,' and so on up to '*ten*.' Both pronounced the last number just as plumply and firmly as the first. When the 'ten' was uttered, the pistols were fired, and both fell! There were about sixty gentlemen at dinner, but two of them only — the landlord, and another man who was brother-in-law to one of the murdered men — left the table. The servants dragged the hunters out into the bar room; and when we went out, after dinner, they were both dead!"

"Now that was pretty cool, all around" said the Colonel to a Mississippian with whom he was talking.

No Northern man, who has never seen men who have been brought up in places where they cannot read and write can imagine how vacant-minded and stupid such men appear. Occasionally we see a man at the North who cannot read, though very seldom among the farmers. But when we do find one so ignorant, he has been associated with men who can read, and he has consequently obtained a good deal of information from them, and he seems much more intelligent than slaveholders do who cannot read themselves, and who have not enjoyed the society of those who can read. I can give no better idea of the impression made on the mind of a Yankee when looking upon a jury made up of such men, than by describing an amusing scene that transpired in court, in the city of D.

A learned physician from Massachusetts, Dr. W., and a shipmaster from Maine, Capt. F., with whom I had a favorable acquaintance during a few weeks stay at D., will excuse this reference to them.

The court house at D., is divided in the center by a railing, three feet high. In one end of the room the court is convened, and the other end is reserved for spectators. There is no seat in the half assigned to the latter, except a narrow seat around the outside of the area. The court was in session at the time of our visit. One of the lawyers was addressing the jury. I was standing near the passage-way in the railing, in the center of the house, and Dr. W. stood near the door, looking upon the court, and listening to the argument of the attorney, when Capt. F. — a stout, rough, sensible, down east sea captain — entered the room, and took a stand by the door near to him. Perceiving there were vacant seats on the court side of the railing, and none very near on our side, the Capt. said to Dr. W.,

"Why can't we go inside, and take a seat?"

"Those seats belong to the jury," replied the Dr.

They were rough, long seats, without backs or desks.

"But that is not the jury," said Capt. F., pointing to the pale, puny looking fellows that occupied those seats.

"Yes it is, Capt.," said Dr. W. "Don't you see? The lawyer is talking to them now."

"I know better than that," said Capt. F., casting a "look for breakers" over them a second time.

He saw that the jury paid little attention to what the lawyer was saying to them. They were talking with each other in little squads of two or three together, in whispers so loud that we could sometimes distinguish the half smothered oath, followed by a copious expectoration of tobacco juice. Capt. F. stepped along to the place where I was standing, and said to me,

"Why can't we go in there and sit down?" pointing to a chance for two on the jury seat.

"Those seats belong to the jury," I replied, "and I suppose the court would object to our taking seats with the jury while the trial is going on."

The Capt. was now compelled to believe that this

was really the jury, though he could not comprehend why men who seemed so ignorant and dissipated, had been selected for such an important trust.

"I would be hung or I would be shot," he exclaimed, "before I would be tried for any thing *great* by such a looking set of fellows as that!"

This was uttered in a whisper so loud that the sheriff, who was at the further end of the room, near the judge, came along and said to us, "You disturb the court, gentlemen! Please retire out there and take a seat," pointing to the seat by the wall.

"Look here, Capt.!" said Capt. F. to the officer, with a peering look, and a thrust of his finger towards the face of the sheriff, "I'll tell you what I will do: I will give you fifty dollars for a true daguerreotype of your jury there!" The officer laughed, and returned to his seat, while Dr. W. and myself started suddenly for the outside, where a hearty laugh would not disturb the court.

I visited a court in L., in March, 1853. Two men were on the jury by the name of Smith — George and Joseph. They were brothers. George Smith was a temperance man — a rare specimen in that locality — but "Joe" was a notorious drunkard. One of the lawyers said to the judge in the morning that Joe Smith was too drunk to perform the duties of a juror, and another must be called to take his place.

"Very well, I will take care of that," replied the judge.

The judge calls the names of the jurors, in some of

the Southern courts, instead of their being called by the clerk, as in the courts of New England. Now George Smith had agreed with Joe to help him into the court house, and Joe was not to attempt to speak when the judge called his name, — as he was one of those unfortunate inebriates who cannot speak distinctly when intoxicated, — but George was to answer for him, with the hope that the judge would not suspect that Joe was not responding himself. When the judge came to the name of Smith, he repeated, in a low, respectful voice,

"George Smith!"

"*Here*, sir," responded George Smith, modestly.

"*Joe Smith!*" vociferated the judge, in a thrilling tone, as if preparing for a stern rebuke.

"Here, sir," answered his proxy, George, in a firm voice.

"*Joe Smith*," said the judge, "I understand that you are drunk, and are not fit to be in the seats with the jury to-day. *How is it?*"

"*'Tis a lie, sir!*" answered George, quickly, with an oath. "I haven't drunk a drop to-day!"

"Oh, 'tis a mistake, I suppose," said the judge, not noticing that Joe did not speak for himself. "I presume it is a mistake, sir, and I hope you will excuse me, Mr. Smith!"

Joe Smith retained his seat with the other jurors, and an indictment against a Mr. W., for an assault with intent to kill, was called up for trial. The evidence was soon "all out," from which it appeared that Mr. W. had for some time a standing quarrel with a neighbor of his, and that during the fight which had brought him into court, he had knocked his neighbor down and cut his throat, though the wound did not prove fatal.

The counsel for the accused pleaded in justification that his client was provoked to the deed by the complainant, by insulting and abusive language.

"And now, gentlemen of the jury," he said, "I put the question to you, as honorable, high minded men, if such a rascal as this complainant had come up to you, as he did to my client, and called you all sorts of insulting names and opprobrious epithets, *would you not have knocked him down?*"

"*Yes! yes!*" responded the jury, all around.

Satisfied with what I had seen, I went on my way, without waiting for the case to be submitted to them by the judge.

A citizen of Tennessee removed to Georgia, and purchased one hundred acres of land near the residence of a wealthy slaveholder. He fenced in his little farm, which was surrounded on all sides by the lands of the slaveholders; and he worked in his field himself, and his sons with him. Thus a free labor system was established in the midst of slaveholders, for this man owned no slaves.

The rich planter who was his neighbor, soon found out that he was setting a dangerous example. A working free man, who sympathized with slaves, who took the liberty to talk with them and ask them if they had enough to eat, and if not, would give them corn from his own crib, affording them little comforts, and expre:

ing grief for their afflictions, could not be endured. The slaveholder became deeply enraged, and watched long for an opportunity to bring some charge against him, that would take away his property and drive him out of the place. At length this poor man's wife was taken sick with a fever, and the neighborhood physician was called.

The slaveholder now conceived a plan to banish his obnoxious neighbor. He went to the physician, Dr. R., and persuaded him to charge the husband of the sick woman several hundred dollars for each visit he should make during the course of that fever, — the common congestive fever of the climate, which usually lasts from seven to ten days. Dr. R. in this way made up a bill of some thirty-five hundred dollars. Payment was refused, and Dr. R. sued the account. The case went to the jury — such a jury as the slaveholders had succeeded in packing — and their verdict was for the whole amount. The defendant was obliged to give up his farm to pay it, and leave his home, penniless, a victim of an institution that makes courts and juries the instruments of its purposes.

The above facts are stated on the authority of two native Georgians, who resided in the same county with the parties, and one of them, a worthy pastor of an evangelical church, attended the court.

XVIII.

SLAVERY HARDENS THE HEART.

"That face of his, the hungry cannibals
Would not have touched, would not have stained with blood;—
But you are more inhuman, more inexorable,
Oh! ten times more than tigers of Hyrcania."

SHAKESPEARE.

PERHAPS the darkest feature, after all, in the system of slavery, is its influence upon the slaveholder, and upon all who become familiar with it. Its sure tendency to harden the heart, to dry up all the fountains of human sympathy, to make one callous to the wrongs and the woes of those around him, is stamped upon the very surface of society throughout the South. One can hardly spend a day there — unless in the luxury of some slaveholder's hospitality he forgets every thing but his own present ease — without being forced to exclaim

"There is no flesh in man's obdurate heart,—
It does not feel for man."

And yet slaveholders themselves are hardly conscious of this. If they are natives of the South, they have always been trained to witness the cruelties incident to the slave system, and they seem to have no conception of any better state of society. If they are emigrants from the North, so gradually has the system gained its control over them, — winding its fatal cords around their hearts, deadening their sensibilities, and familiarizing them to deeds of wrong, and cries of distress, — that they are unconscious of its influence. Northern men who become slaveholders — who once, like Hazael, would have been indignant if some prophet had foretold their deeds — are quite as likely to become cruel masters as those who have been brought up in the slave States.

Sometimes the Northern mind is shocked by an account of some horrid transaction in the South, in which the actors seem more like devils than like men. The story seems so incredible that those who are determined to maintain a good opinion of slaveholders affect to disbelieve it; — while others doubt it not, because they know that often, where slavery exists,

> "deeds are wrought,
> Which well might shame extremest hell."

And yet these things are not doubted or denied in the South. On the contrary they are related with a *nonchalance* and an indifference that are surprising. The slaveholders seem to glory in their shame.

An illustration of this may be seen in the recent burning of a slave in Sumpter county, Alabama, and the manner in which the slaveholders — even those who do not justify it — relate the facts. "Dave," a slave of James D. Thornton, accused of the murder of the daughter of his mistress, was arrested, and confessed his guilt. Mr. Thornton and his friends assembled to the number of one hundred men, well armed, got into the jail by a stratagem, seized the slave, and bore him off in triumph. What followed, I will give in the language of the *Sumpter Whig:*

"*They left in high glee with the prisoner,* whom they felicitated themselves they had captured by a *coup d'etat,* and without a resort to the formidable weapons with which they were armed.

"Just before leaving, some one in the crowd extended an invitation to the Sheriff and the good people of Livingston to appear near the residence of James D. Thornton, (the place of the horrid murder,) at 1 o'clock P. M., on Friday following, to witness the burning of the murderer. In justice to our Sheriff, we will state here, that he and one of his deputies had gone to Wetumpka, to carry Robinson to the penitentiary, who had been sentenced at our last Circuit Court. Indeed, if he had been at home on the occasion, he could not have arrested this unlawful procedure; for the rescue was effected so quick, and with so little noise, that many of our citizens living immediately on the square knew nothing of this affair until next morning. Two of the Sheriff's deputies afterwards demanded the prisoner, and remonstrated against this proceeding, but it was like talking to the winds. Some of our citizens, who went down at the appointed place to witness the burning of the murderer, have related to us that the negro was tied to a stake, with fat light wood piled around him, *and that the torch was applied in the presence of two thousand persons, who had met there to witness the novel scene.* The rumors which got afloat, that the negro was tortured, are entirely untrue."

Not long before I visited Georgia there was a tragedy very much like this in that State, though the details were more shocking. I visited the place where it occurred, and heard it repeated by different persons, — though the story was related to me in all its particulars, as I give it here, by Mrs. A., the wife of a slaveholder, who was compelled by her husband to witness the scene. She was an intelligent, Christian lady, — a native of Augusta, in that State. Like very many Southern women, she was opposed to slavery, and sympathized with the slaves in their sufferings, — and for this reason her harsh, unfeeling husband required her to go with him to see the terrible deed.

A punisment had been inflicted upon this slave by his mistress, which I will not name, or describe. In revenge for it he seized a hatchet, and struck her twice upon the head, inflicting wounds that he supposed would cause instant death, — though she afterwards recovered. If there were any possible justification of the law of retaliation — if revenge ever could be right — he would have been justified in taking the life of his mistress. Had he not been a slave, public sentiment would have pronounced him guiltless. So he felt. Instead of trying to escape, he ran immediately to the court house — where the court was then in session — told the officers what he had done and expressed his willingness to suffer the penalty of the law. That, like those who take life without any excuse, he would, in due course of law, suffer upon the gallows, was what he anticipated. He wished not to avoid the doom. He desired not to live.

But the slaveholders in that region decided that he should suffer a different fate. They determined that he should be burned alive! And they offered him up — a sacrifice — upon the bloody altar of slavery!

They raised money, by subscription, to pay his mistress for her loss. Several persons admitted to me that they contributed for that purpose. The slave was given up to them, and for five days he received fifty lashes each day, upon his naked back, with the heavy "cotton planter's whip." So was his Heavenly Master scourged before his cruel death!

The appointed day, — which some said was Saturday, others Monday, but which my informant said was the Sabbath, — at length arrived, and the multitude assembled. There is a sparse population in that and the adjoining counties, — not over five thousand within a space of thirty miles square; — and yet the number present was variously estimated at from ten to fifteen thousand. All the slaves in all that region were compelled to attend. The slave who was to be executed was the husband of a young wife, and the father of two little daughters, who were also forced to be present! The victim was led out from the place of his confinement to an oak tree, near the court house, where he was surrounded by a vast crowd of beholders, clamoring for the consuming fire! The single garment he had on was taken off, a cord was fastened to the hands, and thus naked, he was drawn up several feet from the earth, and hung suspended upon a large limb.

A slow fire, made of hard pine shavings, was then kindled beneath him. At first the smoke arose and enveloped him, and then the clear, bright flames quickly ascended, coiling about the limbs, encircling the body, scorching the nerves, crisping the fibres, charring the flesh, — and, in mortal anguish, he was, (to use the lady's own language,) "*sweating, as it were, great drops of blood!*" But, before life was entirely extinguished, when he was in the last convulsive agonies of death, the executioners applied their knives, which they had prepared, fastened upon poles, cutting open the thorax and abdomen! Then one of the fiends thrust in a hook, prepared in like manner, and dragged out the heart! Another tore out the liver! A third wrenched out the lungs! And with these vital organs, elevated above their heads on the poles, they ran through the crowd screaming, "*So shall it be done to the slave that murders his mistress!*"

Then the heart was thrown upon the ground — and the crowd rushed over it, forward and backward, stamping upon it, crushing out the life blood, treading it in the dust. Then, in like manner, the lungs, and the liver were disposed of, amid the deafening shouts of the savage throng. "Such a fiendish, devilish yell," said my informant, "was never heard this side of Satan's kingdom!"

I know that this story is too shocking, almost, for

belief. And yet, after careful inquiry, on the very ground where it transpired, I was fully satisfied of its truth. Without any coloring of my own, "I tell it as it was told to me" by one who was an unwilling witness of it all. How terrible the lesson it teaches of the influence of slavery upon those who are connected with it!

"The slaves," says the Kentucky Synod of the Presbyterian church, "suffer all that can be inflicted upon them by *insane anger*." There is much meaning in this expression. To fully understand the influence of slavery on the slaveholder, we must see him at home — see how excitable, how changeful, how impulsive, how irritable he is.

I never met an individual who seemed to abhor slavery more profoundly, than Mrs. A., — the lady whom I have already mentioned. Nor did I become acquainted with any slaveholder who hated the anti-slavery cause more deeply than her proud, but generous, and high-spirited husband. I passed several days with that family. As soon as Mrs. A. ascertained my views of slavery, she freely told me her own bitter experience.

"Slavery destroys the temper of every body connected with it," said this lady. "Slaveholders' children, instead of being taught to govern their tempers, are encouraged to indulge their passions; and, thus educated, they become the slaves of passion. Those masters who are the most kind and benevolent when free from the influence of anger, often become the most cruel and merciless when under its control."

This fact was forcibly exemplified in that family. I

was riding in the stage one day in company with Mr. A. While passing a slave hut, which was a few rods from the road, Mr. A. requested the driver to stop a few minutes. As he was descending from the carriage, I saw him put a five dollar note in his vest pocket. He ran towards the hut, but before he reached it, an old, grey-headed negress came out and walked rapidly to meet him. When they met, he threw his arms around her neck, and kissed her, — and she locked her arms about his neck, and kissed him! They talked together a few minutes, when he gave her the five dollar bill, and hastened back to the coach. The good, old, black slave mother followed after him, invoking the blessings of Heaven upon him.

"I suppose you think," said Mr. A. to me, laughing, as he was resuming his seat in the coach, "that you have seen something strange this time, sir?"

"I do, indeed," I replied; and I added, playfully, — "but I have often heard of such things among slaveholders."

"Let me explain, sir," said Mr. A. "The manifestation of attachment you have witnessed between that good woman and myself, is really the affection between a parent and child. Not that I am her son. But my own mother was an unnatural mother. She used to whip me terribly, and she treated me with great cruelty in every respect. This slave mother nursed me when I was an infant; and whenever she saw my own mother abuse me, she would take me up in her arms, and carry me away to her little hut, to soothe me, and caress me. I soon loved her more than I did my own mother. I have always continued to love her better than my own mother! And she says that I have always treated her so kindly, and affectionately, that she loves me as much as she does either of her own sons. She says she means to kiss me every time we meet as long as she lives, unless I forbid it; and I tell you, sir, that I shall never have it in my heart to do so; for I know I shall want to kiss her every time I see her, as long as she lives."

A few days afterwards, I mentioned this occurrence to Mrs. A., and expressed my surprise to see such signs of affection between her husband and that old slave.

"You may be assured," remarked the lady, with evident delight at the fact, "that there was nothing feigned in that matter. I know my husband loves that good woman truly, and that she merits it justly. I have been with him many a time to see her, and he always gives her money and other presents. She will never suffer for any comfort while he lives. She is kindly treated where she is, and she has her kindred about her."

"But these slaveholders are strange men!" she added, mournfully — "so kind one moment — so cruel the next. You would infer that my husband, judging only from what you have seen, is one of the best hearted men in the world, — and that he would never treat a slave cruelly, would you not, sir?"

"Most certainly," I replied. "Is he not so?"

"Very tender hearted and benevolent; indulgent to a fault, sir, except when his anger is excited. But then, he seems to be beside himself, he is so cruel and merciless. His passions run away with him. They were never restrained while he was young, and now they control him. I will show you the proof of his inhumanity when in a passion.

She called in, from the kitchen, an old slave girl by the name of "Sylva." She was so old that she recollected scenes in the Revolutionary war. She was the cook for Mr. A.'s father, had been for his grandfather before him, and was still the cook in the family of the third generation.

"Take off your shoes, Sylva," said Mrs. A., "and let this gentleman see your feet."

"I don't want to," said Sylva.

"But I want you to," said her mistress.

"I don't care if you do," replied Sylva, sullenly.

"*You must*," said the mistress, firmly.

The fear of punishment impelled her to remove the shoes. *Four toes* on one foot, and *two* on the other, were wanting!

"There!" said the mistress; "my husband, who learned the blacksmith's trade for the purpose of teaching it to his slaves, to increase their market value, has, with his own hands, pounded off, and wrung off all those toes, when insane with passion. And it was only last week that he thought Sylva was saucy to me, and he gave her thirty lashes with the horse whip. She was so old that I could not bear to see it, and I left the house."

"Sylva says," Mrs. A. continued, "that she has been the mother of thirteen children, every one of whom she destroyed with her own hands, in their infancy, rather than have them suffer in slavery!"

It so happened, that before the day passed, I had an opportunity to see the effects of the system upon the temper of Mrs. A. herself. I had a temperance lecture announced at the village, two miles distant, at six o'clock that evening. Sylva was the only cook, at that time, in the kitchen. A little past four o'clock, Mrs. A. stepped to the door and told her that I was going to the village at sunset, and wanted an early supper. But Sylva was "sulky," after the talk about her toes had opened her wounds afresh, and she did not feel disposed to gratify her mistress. Mrs. A. continued to call to her more frequently, and more earnestly, until the time drew near for me to leave. I began to suspect that the cook was intending to disappoint us, and, at a quarter before six, I said to the lady,—

"I think I will prefer to go down to the lecture, madam, and take supper after I return."

"O that will be too bad," replied Mrs. A. "You will be famished and exhausted."

She went to the door again, and in a nervous, earnest, impatient tone, she said—

"Sylva! Wont the cake do to bring in now?"

"Not *quite* done yet, mistress! I'll bring it in by and by,"—was the provoking reply.

And now, even this amiable lady, with all her dignity and self respect, lost the control of her temper, and screamed out at the top of her voice—

"I sometimes wish *thunder and lightning* would come down that chimney, and see if that would not stir you up a little!"

I laughed immoderately. Mrs. A. turned towards me, clenched her hands, the tears rolling down her cheeks, —

"O dear!" she exclaimed, "you don't know what provocations we have!"

"Yes I do know, madam! for I have seen them," I replied; "and I have wondered at your patience."

"So you see, now, it is as I told you," said Mrs. A., sadly. "Slavery ruins the temper of everybody connected with it."

"The slaveholder's wife and daughters suffer most," she continued, after becoming composed, "and if the women of the North only knew what we are compelled to suffer, they would all be Mrs. Stowes."

"If the *women* of Georgia had the privilege of deciding the question of slavery," said Mrs. A. to me, at another time, "I am certain that it would not live until sunset."

"Yet I suppose, madam," said I, "that few of them would dare publicly express their hatred of the system?"

"By no means, sir," she answered quickly, "for we scarcely venture to speak our thoughts, even to our husbands."

She then spoke of the poverty and wretchedness of the poor white people in the South.

"Are the whites so poor and destitute that they frequently suffer from hunger?" I inquired.

"No one has any idea," she replied, "of the poverty of this class; and nobody seems to care for them."

"I have always heard," said I, "that slaveholders are

proverbially benevolent and hospitable, even to strangers; and therefore I supposed that they would not let their neighbors suffer from any want in their power to supply."

"They are hospitable to each other, and to strangers," said Mrs. A. "But the poor at their own doors, if not slaveholders, are left unnoticed, and uncared for."

The prevailing habit of intemperance in the South is another source of much cruel treatment. Men whose passions, even when they are sober, are ever ready to kindle to a flame, are like maniacs, when intoxicated. And slaveholders, as a class, are addicted to the excessive use of intoxicating liquors.

A slaveholder by the name of Austin — a very kind man when he was sober — when in a drunken fit, killed a favorite slave by the name of "Alexander."

When intoxicated, every object had, to his view, an illusory aspect. He would fancy, at such times, that his children were not his own. And his neighbors' slaves, in his diseased imagination, took the places of his own. This state of mind is peculiar to a certain class of inebriates.

His neighbor W. owned a slave boy, "Joe," who was very vicious. Austin had notified Joe's master to keep him at home, but he neglected to do it. Joe afterwards committed a crime on Austin's plantation. Austin went to the master, and informed him of it, — and he told him that if he ever again found that slave on his premises he would shoot him. In a short time after this Austin came home from the tavern intoxicated. And seeing his own faithful slave, "Alexander," coming in at his gate, he thought it was the culprit, "Joe," whom he had banished from his premises.

"Joe," exclaimed Austin, "what are you in here for again, you scoundrel?"

"It is not Joe, master," replied Alexander, "it is I. Don't you know 'Alick,' master?"

"I know Alick; he 's a good boy," said Austin; "and I know you, Joe! you black villain!"

"Look here, master Austin! strange you don't know"—

"Didn't I tell you I would kill you if I found you in here again?" persisted Austin;—and he ran towards the slave, staggering as he went, and drawing his long knife. The slave not daring to resist, fled to his cabin. The master pursued, rushed in, and commenced cutting him with the knife, until Alexander, to save his life, wrenched it from his hand. Austin then went to his house, seized his gun, and returning to Alexander's cabin, shot him!

I came from Darien up to Savannah on Friday, in the spring of 1853, and took lodgings at my former home, the Marshall House. On Saturday I walked about the city—renewing old acquaintances—visiting the market, the post-office, the reading rooms, stores, commission houses, &c.,—but I received no intimation that a murder had been committed in that city a day or two previous. At the Marshall House I found many of the old boarders with whom I was acquainted. I attended church with them the next Sabbath,—but I heard no one speak of any murder. On Monday morning I step ped into the office of a gentleman of high standing, who went from Massachusetts, and he gave me a cordial greeting.

"I suppose," remarked my friend, "that you have heard of the murder of "Cuffee," by Wilson?"

"I have not, sir," said I.

"Why! When did you come into the city?"

"Last Friday."

"Well, where have you been in the mean time, that you have not heard of that terrible murder?"

I informed him of my facilities to obtain news — stating where I had been and whom I had seen.

"Now this is astonishing," said my friend, "that a man can be killed in one of our public streets, in broad daylight, and the fact not be known at the market, or the reading rooms, or the hotels!"

"Don't your papers publish such accounts?" I inquired.

"No sir. I looked in the daily papers Friday and Saturday, and I was surprised to see no mention of it there."

"Can you give me the facts, sir?" said I.

"O, yes," replied the merchant, promptly. And he added, "I suppose you know Wilson?"

"I do not, sir. I have merely seen him, — but have no acquaintance with him."

"Did you know Cuffee?" he asked.

"I did not."

"Cuffee was a house carpenter, a very smart, ingenious, industrious workman. He hired his time of his master, for which he paid him two hundred and seventy-five dollars a year. He did job-work, and by constant, hard labor, could earn a little more than the amount paid his master, and thus have the means of affording a few comforts to his wife and family, which they would not otherwise enjoy. You see that window, sir!"—pointing to a large window in his office.—"Cuffee put in that window a few days since. He made the sash, and the frame, and put up those neat little fixtures you see at the sides."

"About six months ago," continued Mr. ——, "Cuffee did some work for Wilson which was worth at least ten dollars. He waited some time for his pay, but Wilson neglected it. Cuffee asked him two or three times for it, and Wilson refused as often to pay him. Last week Cuffee met him in the street and demanded payment.

'I have been sick lately, Mr. Wilson,' said Cuffee, 'and I have not collected quite enough to pay the amount due to my master; and if you ever intend to pay me for the work I did for you I will thank you to do it now.'

'The work was not half done,' replied Wilson; 'and I thought I shouldn't pay you any thing for it.'

Two gentlemen were standing on the side-walk, who saw and heard it all.

'Well,' said Cuffee, 'remember that I shall never ask you for it again, so you will decide it finally this time.'

Wilson took a half dollar from his pocket, and held it out towards Cuffee, in his open hand.

'Is that all you mean to pay me, Mr. Wilson?' exclaimed Cuffee, contemptuously.

'Yes,' replied Wilson, angrily,—'take that, or nothing.'

'Why Mr. Wilson! that is not half as much as I paid a boy who helped me do the job.'

'I don't care for that,' said Wilson; 'that is all I shall pay you.'

'Mr. Wilson,' said Cuffee, much excited, 'if we were a little nearer the river, I would throw this half dollar into it, just to let you know that I can live without it, and that I despise your meanness and dishonesty.'

Now it does not answer for a slave to call a slaveholder mean and dishonest. No matter how mean and dishonest he may be, the slave must not remind him of it. Wilson commenced beating, kicking, and cursing the slave. The spectators did not interfere — perhaps they dared not provoke the murderer's wrath. Cuffee was able to defend himself, if public opinion would have sustained him; — he could have run from the assassin, but he feared the bullet would overtake him.

The blows continued to fall upon him so thick and heavy, that, under a consciousness of his innocence, having more moral courage than if he had not been making his own contracts, and thinking, probably, that he could fall back on his kind master for protection, he straightened himself up, stepped back, stretched out his stalwart arm, and exclaimed —

'I tell you now, Mr. Wilson, that if I was not a slave, I would not endure such treatment as this from you for a moment!'

Behold him lifting his hand against a white man! Unpardonable offense! Any man may kill him with impunity! Wilson drew his double barrelled pistol, and shot the noble hearted slave dead on the spot!

The Supreme Court was in session in that city at the time. Cuffee's master felt indignant that his faithful servant had been stricken down under such circumstances, and he entered a complaint against Wilson for the murder. But on receiving a thousand dollars as a compensation for his value, he abandoned the prosecution; and the murderer still goes abroad, unpunished!

While I was in Georgia a shocking murder was committed in Clark county. The following account of it is from the *Savannah Morning News*, of the 26th of January, 1853.

"On Thursday last, James Clark, a well known citizen of Clark county, made an assault upon his negro woman, for a cause which we have not heard stated. He then ordered her into the corner, and commenced pitching his knife at her, point foremost. As the knife would enter her flesh, he would compel the victim to draw it out, and return it to him. This demoniacal amusement was continued until the slave was covered with about fifty bleeding gashes. The same day he whipped his wife, cut her all over the head with his knife, not dangerously, we understand, but in a mass of cruel and painful punctures. He also cut off her eyelids. This drama wound up, on Friday last, by the commission of a murder. Clark on that day ordered his wife to go and call Lewis, (a negro belonging to the family.) She obeyed,—but the slave refused to come, through dread of his enraged master, we suppose. Mrs. Clark returned, and was whipped by her husband, for not bringing the negro! Five times was she sent upon this capricious mission, five times was it fruitless, and each time was she whipped for her failure. Clark then called to the slave, informing him that he would shoot him the next morning. The negro, it seems, did not heed the warning, for while splitting rails the next day, he was deliberately shot by his master. The wound was fatal; the negro ran about three hundred yards, and fell in mortal agony. Thus terminated one of the most barbarous transactions that it has ever been our painful and repugnant duty to record."

One day while conversing with Mr. C., the city marshal of Darien, upon matters of this kind, he related to me the following thrilling story. The facts were within his own personal knowledge.

Charles Pelot owned a slave — "Cato," — the best pilot in that port. Every shipmaster who visited Darien, felt perfectly safe in entering the harbor, however thick the fog, or violent the storm, if Cato was at the helm. He was remarkably intelligent, and faithful; and of course he was valuable to his master for that reason. Everybody knew him, and had perfect confidence in him. His master owned no other slave, — and he indulged Cato, giving him privileges which were not granted to other slaves. Though it was not allowed by law, Cato was permitted to take a gun, and go out among the islands in pursuit of game. His services as pilot were often in demand, at a high price, — so that he almost or quite supported his master's family.

Cato's family belonged to a master residing in that city, who neglected properly to supply their wants. He was, therefore, generously permitted to visit them often, carry them food, and clothing, and take care of them in sickness.

It so happened that Mr. Pelot sold his property in Darien, with the intention of removing to Jacksonville, in Florida. Slaveholders never consult their slaves in business matters, no matter how intelligent they may be. Cato, therefore, remained in ignorance of his master's purpose, until the evening before he was expecting to leave the city.

Mr. C. told me that he happened to be present when Cato's master informed him of his centemplated removal.

"Cato!" said he, "I have sold my property here, and am going down to Jacksonville."

"When are you going, master?" inquired the slave, his voice trembling, as if all the fears of a lifetime were crowding upon him in this single moment.

"I am going to-morrow," replied Mr. P.

"Do you want me to go with you, master?" inquired the already wretched slave.

"Yes, Cato!" said the master. "You know I depend upon your labor for the support of my family. I want you for a pilot at Jacksonville."

"Are you going to buy my wife and children, master?"

Cato's emotions were so strong, and his anxiety so intense, that he could hardly ask the question. A moment of awful silence passed — the master could not speak, and the slave, as if encouraged by his delay to reply, added —

"Now if you will buy Nelly and the children, master Pelot, I should like to go with you; for you have always been good to me, and I don't want to leave you!"

"I wish for your sake, Cato, that I could buy Nelly and the little girls, — but I am not able," replied Pelot, sadly, and with evident sorrow of heart for the wretched family.

"Well, then, I can't go with you, master," said Cato.

"You must go, Cato," replied the master; "you are all my dependence for a living."

"I tell you I can't go, master, and leave my wife and children in the hands of that man! You *know*, master!" said Cato, pointing towards the defenceless hut where his unprotected family lived.

"I *do know*, Cato," said the sympathizing master, "and I pity you! But I cannot buy your family, and I cannot part with you. You must be ready to start with us in the morning." — The slave folded his arms upon his breast, raised his eyes to Heaven, as if imploring Divine assistance, and then he said to his master, firmly,—

"You have always been kind to me, master Pelot. I love you, and would like to go with you, — but I will never go away from Darien, and leave my wife and children in the hands of that man! *I have resolved to die first!*"

This seeming defiance of his authority enraged the master, and anger took the place of pity.

"You will go with me, to-morrow morning!" he exclaimed.

Cato loaded his old rusty rifle, and fled that night to the woods. In the morning, Mr. C., the city marshal, was ordered to pursue him. He told me that he kept hounds for that purpose. He went out behind the court house, — which stands outside of the city, near the pine woods, — and Cato called to him from the top of a tree —

"Don't you come to take me, Mr. C.! You know I told master Pelot that I would die before I would leave Darien, and let my wife and children suffer as they would. I knew it was no use to run away, for the dogs would catch me; and I don't want to hurt you, Mr. C.; but I will shoot the first man that comes to take me!"

Mr. C. returned, and told Pelot that he would have nothing to do with taking Cato, — not even if he should be removed from his office for this decision. But there were two desperados in that city, who volunteered to go and take him. The name of one of them was Sam. Blunt.

"Bring him in, *dead or alive*!" said Pelot, when they started.

Blunt had a longer rifle than Cato had. The two man-hunters went out around the court house, when Cato admonished them of their danger if they advanced farther. Blunt raised his rifle, and fired! Cato fell to the ground. They took him up, — but he was dead!!!

B. S., of F. H., in South Carolina, owned a giant slave whose name was Dread. This slave was represented to me by one of the neighbors as a man of superior strength, both of body and mind, being nearly seven feet in height. There were forty slaves at work on the plantation of B. S., before Dread was added to the number; and this name was given him by the new master on account of his uncommon physical strength.

The next year Dread was made overseer of the gang, and the management of the plantation was wholly left to his care. The farm was well conducted under his supervision, and every thing went on smoothly and prosperously for several years. The task of every hand was always well and seasonably performed, without whipping. If a feeble woman was sick, or unable to accomplish her task alone, her husband or brother was allowed to assist her. Or if a weak, feeble man could not keep up with the gang, his friend was permitted to help him. This is a privilege not customarily granted to slaves.

The fields of B. S. were now so much more productive than those of others around him, that the neighboring planters frequently sought advice of his colored overseer, in relation to the management of their farms; thus deferring to his opinion, and admitting that he possessed more practical knowledge of agricultural matters than either themselves or their white overseers.

A gentleman, well acquainted with Dread, told me that he regarded him not only as much the stoutest, but the most intellectual man he ever saw.

"Dread had the largest head," he remarked, "I have ever seen, — and I have seen Daniel Webster; and his natural abilities were not inferior to those of that statesman."

Placed in a condition less humble than most slaves, he had never appeared so menial and timid. He felt and acted more like a free man. He did not always take off his cap and put it under his arm whenever he met a white man in the street, or entered his dwelling.

It was natural that the white overseers on the surrounding plantations should be jealous of his success. And soon it began to be whispered around the neighborhood that, if Dread were so disposed, he might become a leader in an insurrection.

The slaveholders held a conference, and decided that it was necessary for B. S. to make an experiment that would test the manhood of the giant slave, and ascertain whether he could be made as submissive as all slaves should be made, to insure the safety of the masters. Among the plans that were suggested to B. S., one was to obtain another overseer, and put Dread to work under him in the gang; and if he expressed the least objection to the change, to whip him severely, and "*break him in.*"

A large, tall, stout Yankee was secured for a driver, and Dread was ordered to take his hoe, and perform his task with the other hands. Without expressing the least surprise or regret at the loss of his place, or even presuming to inquire why he was to be no longer overseer, he went to work with as much apparent cheerfulness as usual.

This was so unexpected, that the masters were greatly

perplexed. They could really find no fault in the slave on which to predicate a charge and inflict a punishment. His noble, fearless bearing, and stately step, were unmistakeable signs that he felt altogether too manly and independent for a humble slave; but how to develope his feelings and prove the fact, was the difficult question. There was nothing in his character or conduct that deserved the slightest reproof, much less a punishment sufficiently severe to crush his manhood and break his invincible spirit. Still all agreed that something must be done.

Finally, they concluded to prefer false charges against him, and punish him if he complained of suffering wrongfully. The master treated him with unusual severity. One, among numerous complaints brought against him, was that he did not hoe his corn so well as the other hands. To remove this, Dread performed a double task, — hoeing two rows to each of the others one. Tom, who hoed next to Dread, told me that Dread removed every weed, hoed it as neat as a garden, determined to remove every cause for complaint; for he saw that a terrible storm was arising upon him.

Dread and Tom occupied the same hut after the new overseer had come; and they had always been mutual friends.

"Master S.," said Tom, who related the story to me, "came into our hut one evening, soon after we had finished work, looking so pale that he frightened me; and he said,

"'Dread! I say you don't hoe your corn so well as the other hands.'

'How do you know that, master!' "replied the intrepid slave, rising up respectfully from his low stool, and looking the master calmly in the eye."

"Now I knew," said Tom, "that master S. had not been into the field that day. Nor had he seen the overseer, as his quarters were beyond our hut, and further from the house. Besides, had he consulted the overseer, he would have been informed that, instead of not doing his work 'as well,' Dread had done his work better, and twice as much, as either of the other hands. But the moment he questioned his master's knowledge, he had exceeded the prerogative of a slave, and this threw his master into a violent fit of anger."

'Ah! you have got *above* yourself, boy,' he vociferated, raging and foaming with passion. 'I must have you *taken down a notch!* You shall be flogged, you impudent, black rascal!'

'*I shall not receive a flogging*, sir!' "replied the indignant slave, firmly and fearlessly."

"Mr. S. then ran out to the overseer, and told him to call out all the hands."

'Now take him and tie him,' "said Mr. S., when the whole gang had assembled in front of Dread's hut, and he was standing in the door. This," said Tom, "they attempted to do, in a scuffle which lasted nearly an hour; but they were not able for a moment to confine one of his limbs; for with his hands and feet he flung them on the ground as fast as they came near him. He evidently avoided injuring the slaves more than was absolutely necessary, in defending himself; for he knew they all loved him."

Soon after this fruitless effort to subdue Dread, the master and overseer of another plantation were employed to come and help bind and whip him. In the mean time, Dread furnished himself with a long butcher-knife, with which he felt secure. When he saw them coming into the field to take him, he dropped his hoe, drew the rude weapon from his side, advanced a few steps towards them, and brandished the knife, as he stood in an attitude of conscious innocence, moral courage, physical strength, and bold defiance of his foes!

"No man," said Tom, "dared lay a finger on him!"

Now a crisis had come.—A slave had successfully resisted his master. This must not be tolerated. Such an insurrectionary spirit must be crushed—cost what it may. The deadly purpose was formed in the heart of the master.

"The gun was loaded," said Tom, "and I was ordered to take the ammunition, and accompany my master."

'What are you going to do *now*?' "said Mrs. S. to her husband, as he was passing out of the house."

'I am going out on a squirrel hunt,' "replied Mr. S., with apparent composure."

"Had mistress known his intention to kill Dread," said Tom, "I think she would have dissuaded him from his bloody purpose,—for she was a Christian woman. But we started off before she had time to say more. Passing around behind the house, we came in sight of the slaves at work in a plum orchard, in the valley behind the hill. Master raised his gun — held it steady to his eye, until the victim was selected from the other hands, — and then he fired!"

A heavy charge of buck shot was lodged in the thigh of the great-hearted, unconquerable Dread. The large artery was divided. The blood poured from the wound. Dread ran out a few rods to the hill side, crying to Heaven for vengeance on his murderer, and uttering, in deep, thunder tones, that seemed to make the earth tremble beneath him,

"I'm killed! I'm killed!! I'm killed!!!"

His devoted wife, who, a moment before, stood laboring faithfully at his side, was the first to reach him, crying in a wild, frantic voice —

"*Dread is dead!* DREAD IS DEAD!! DREAD IS DEAD!!!

"Hold your tongue!" commanded the murderer.

"Still she screamed," said Tom, "louder than I ever before heard from woman — 'Dread is dead! — Dread is dead!'

"The master ran up to the fence, pulled off a rail, and struck that woman with it on the head, repeating — with a horrid oath —

'*Hold your tongue, I say!*'"

This is the "moderate correction" which the laws of the slave States allow! So does slavery harden the heart, until the man is made — not a brute, but — a fiend! So has many a *moral hero* in the South fallen a victim to its cruel, insatiable spirit!

The body of Dread was carried to its *rest*, by his mourning companions. The darkness of night could not cover their sorrow. His heart-stricken wife, broken down with grief which no tongue can describe, was sold a few days afterwards to a "soul-driver" from Kentucky!

XIX.

SLAVERY AND EDUCATION.

"And such is man — a soil which breeds
Or sweetest flowers, or vilest weeds;
Flowers lovely as the morning's light, —
Weeds deadly as an aconite;
Just as the heart is trained to bear
The poisonous weed or floweret fair."

BOWRING.

In the census report of 1850 the disastrous influences of slavery are visible on almost every page. It is true that there are many features not to be found there. The relative amount of manufactures and of commerce have to be sought for from other sources, and, when found, show that the South, with far greater resources, is vastly inferior to the North. But the statistics of the last census exhibit evidence enough to convince any candid mind of the dangers that impend over our nation. From the general fact that the slave States, with much the larger territory, far surpassing the North in fertility of soil, in mildness of climate, with abundance of harbors, and rivers, and waterfalls, for commerce, navigation, and manufactures, have not half so great a free white population as the free States, down to the minutest details of educational institutions, the premature decay of the one, and the rapid growth and prosperity of the other, are written in lines that cannot be overlooked.

In the 15 free States, excluding California, there were 4,742,000 white children between 5 and 20 years of age. Of these, 3,111,000 were returned as scholars attending the various primary schools. In the slave States the number of free white children between 5 and 20 years of age was 2,450,000, and only 974,000 of these were reported as scholars attending any of the schools. There were more scholars in Massachusetts, than in North Carolina, South Carolina, and Georgia. There were more in Maine, than in Virginia, South Carolina, and Mississippi. There were more in either *two* of New York, Ohio, and Pennsylvania, than in all the slave States put together.

Compare Maine with Georgia and North Carolina. In *Maine*, the white population in 1850 was 581,813. Of these, 31,695 were foreigners. The adult population, over 20 years old, was 293,422. Of these, only 6,282 were unable to read and write, and 4,148 of these were foreigners, only 2,134 being native born.

In *Georgia*, the free white population was 521,572, of which only 6,452 were foreigners. There were 217,774 over 20 years old, of whom 41,667 were not able to read or write; and only 406 of these were foreigners, 41,261 being native born.

In *North Carolina* the free white population was 553,028, only 2,565 of whom were foreigners. The number over 20 years old was 241,022, of whom 80,423 could neither read nor write. And of these only 340 were foreigners, 80,83 being native born.

Compare Massachusetts and Virginia. In *Massachusetts* the white population was 985,450. Foreigners, 165,598. The number of adults over 20 years of age, 568,533. Of these, the number not able to read and write was 28,345, of whom 26,484 were foreigners, only 1,861 being native born!

While in *Virginia* the free white population was 894,800, with only 22,593 foreigners. The number over 20 years old was 413,418, of whom 88,520 could not read or write. And of these only 1,137 were foreigners, 87,383, being native born!

The number of *daily newspapers* returned, not including the District of Columbia or California, was 245. Of these, 173 were published in the free States, and 72 in the slave States. The number of weekly newspapers was 1,888,—in the North 1,351, in the South 537! The number in *Massachusetts* was 126, in *Virginia* 55. The number in *New York* was 308, and in *Pennsylvania* 261, being 32 more in these two States, than in all the slave States.

The annual income of the public schools in the thirty States, excluding California and the District of Columbia, from taxation and all other sources, was $ 9,561,859. Of this, $ 6,840,488 is put to the credit of the free States, and only $ 2,721,371 to the slave States. The amount in *Massachusetts* was $ 1,006,795, in *Virginia*

$314,625. In *New York* it was $1,472,657, and in *Pennsylvania* $1,414,530, being $165,816 more in these two States than in all the slave States!!!

Before relating any of my own personal observations, I will allude to some of the reasons that have been given for this disparity between the North and the South. It has been said that they cannot sustain schools in the slave States, on account of the "sparseness of the population." But Maine stands ahead of every other State in the proportion of her children *attending school*, and only one other State equals it in the proportion of her population who can read and write. But there are a less number of inhabitants to the square mile in this State than in Georgia, Virginia, Kentucky, Tennessee, or either of the Carolinas. And a comparison of either of these States with Vermont or New Hampshire shows the same result.

And though, as I shall show, the sparsely settled districts in the South are generally the most noted for the ignorance of the people, it is far otherwise in the North. In the rural districts of New England, among the farmers, the schools are uniformly the best, and the number of ignorant men less than in the cities and the large seaboard towns. I believe the conviction at the North is, that *slaveholders* themselves are generally educated; and that those who cannot read and write are found among the poor non-slaveholding whites and blacks. But it is not so. The non-slaveholders are ignorant and degraded, but not more so than the Crackers. So far as I observed, the slaveholders in the planting districts are quite as destitute of learning as the poor whites; and I have seen a private letter from a colporteur, in which he affirms that he traveled 20 miles in —— county, called on 21 families of slaveholders, and found only two — a man and his wife — who could read.

The slave States are divided into counties only, and not into towns like the free States. Near the center of each county, usually, is the "county seat," where are the court house, jail, church, and school. When other villages spring up, in other parts of the county, they receive adventitious names, until they add a few hundred inhabitants, to enable them to maintain a municipal government, and they then become cities. Some of these cities have less than five hundred inhabitants.

At most of the county seats, schools — called academies — have been established. The standard of education in these academies has always been far below that of the common schools in the New England States. I visited several academies, and in none of them were reading, writing, and arithmetic so thoroughly taught as they are in the common schools of Maine and New Hampshire.

Within a few years the slaveholders themselves, especially those who went from the North, have lost all confidence in the old academy as a suitable school for their children; and hence the recent establishment of four male and eight female colleges, in the cities of Georgia, which are mainly sustained by these Northern men, and instructed by teachers from the North. The standard of education in these colleges is about the same as in the common schools in New England. The *ornamental* branches are better taught, but the *solid,* not so well.

The slaveholders are evidently discouraged by the unsuccessful efforts to educate their *sons.* Hence the number of *female* colleges is double that of *male.* Three of these colleges are under the auspices of the Baptist, three of the Methodist, and two of the Presbyterian denomination. There are from one to two hundred young ladies in these schools. Some of them are from the North, but a large proportion of them are Southern ladies, though the daughters of parents who went from the free States. Most of these young ladies, as well as their teachers, a large proportion of whom are directly from the free States, become the wives of the most wealthy and the best educated slaveholders. The class of literary slaveholders is very small; but they often seek Northern ladies for wives, appreciating their superior literary and intellectual endowments, and their domestic qualifications.

The young *men* who go South to teach, or to engage in the practice of any literary profession, often become connected by marriage with the families of wealthy slaveholders, and then they are generally advocates of slavery.

It is impossible to maintain as good government in the schools in the slave States as we have in the free States. There is not that substantial family discipline maintained, and the salutary home influence in the South, that are every where seen in New England. The slaveholder does not return home from his haunts of dissipation, or his amusements, and gather his family around the fireside, to converse with them about their welfare, and the interests of society, like the Northern farmer, merchant, or mechanic, when the labors of the day are finished.

It is a proverb in New England, that where the children are not governed at home, they cannot, without trouble, be made to mind in school. This is lamentably verified in the schools of the South. The child of the slaveholder is taught to resist every insult, every aggression upon his rights, with physical force, and, if need be, with a fatal weapon. He is instructed to regard a "coward" as the meanest, most odious character in the world, and he shuns no danger to avoid such an opprobrious epithet. Thus the son is often first sent to the pistol gallery, before he is taught to read.

I was in company with a learned physician from Massachusetts, sitting under a tree near an academy in Georgia, when five boys, just dismissed from school, commenced pitching knives at a tree. Two of these boys, whose names were George and John, had a falling out. George took up a piece of limestone, as large as his fist, and threw it with great violence towards John, who was standing near a large oak tree. When John saw the stone coming directly towards him, he sprang behind the tree.

"There John! you mean coward!" said George, contemptuously; "dodge behind a tree, eh! You mean dog! I'll have nothing more to say to you!"

George turned and walked off the play ground, with that air peculiar to a slaveholder, as though the earth were too mean for such a hero to tread. The other three boys repeated George's words, exclaiming simultaneously,

"You are a mean coward, John! Dodge behind a tree! Afraid of a little stone, are you? We'll never play with you again."

And they all started off after the hero George, and left poor disconsolate Johnny standing behind the tree, speechless, motionless, disgraced.

Let that scene be repeated the next day, and Johnny would not dodge the stone. He would not endure another frown of public opinion like that, and thus lose the confidence and companionship of all his little comrades. He will "stand his ground" the next time—and then, as he advances in years, he will take the knife, and, at last, the bullet, preferring *death* to the name and disgrace of a *coward*.

These habits of resistance are carried into the schools, and oppose wholesome restraint there. One of the female teachers in a slave State informed me that she had a boy in her school only eight years of age, who had transgressed an important rule of the school, and she ordered him to come up to the desk. The little fellow drew his knife, and defied her to punish him. She waited sometime, until the boy was off his guard, when she caught him by the arm, dragged him out of his seat, and inflicted the punishment.

Immediately after this, a brother of this lad, only ten

years of age, openly violated the same law, and she commanded him to come forward. She said that she did not suspect there was a pistol in her school, until this boy thrust his hand over behind his head, and pulled out a pistol from under the neck of his jacket, cocked it, pointed it towards her, and exclaimed,

"Now ferule *me*, if you dare!"

In the evening this teacher visited the family, and inquired of the father of those boys how he wished her to manage them.

"I can beat my boys enough at home, madam," was his insulting reply.

A friend of mine from Maine—a graduate of Bowdoin College—is teaching in Tennessee. I recently saw a letter which this young gentleman wrote to his father, in which he stated that twice during the last term, when he attempted to punish boys belonging to his academy, they had drawn pistols upon him, and he was unable to inflict the punishment.

The murder of Mr. Butler, in Kentucky, by Ward, whose acquittal I have already alluded to as illustrating the administration of justice in the South, shows how difficult it is for a teacher, in the slave States, to maintain that discipline without which no school is of much value. The facts are so well known that I need not repeat them. A similar case has lately occurred in another slave State, an account of which I copy from the *Nashville Whig* of June 18th.

"We learn, from a gentleman who was an eye-witness, the following particulars of a most horrible and tragical affair that occurred at Pontotoc, Miss., on Monday last. It appears that Mr. Brown, the principal of the male academy at Pontotoc, had punished one of his pupils about a week since. A brother of the boy that was whipped, by the name of Wray, made threats against Mr. Brown for the aforesaid punishment, to which but little attention was paid. On Monday, young Wray, a youth some seventeen or eighteen years old, took a position where Mr. Brown would pass on his way home from school, and waited until he came along, when Wray attacked him.

The two clinched, Brown only acting in self defense, and those who saw it thought it only to be a scuffle between them, until they saw Brown run a few yards, his hands upon his abdomen, and fall down lifeless. While they were clinched, Wray had inflicted two wounds upon Brown with a large bowie knife, which killed him almost instantly."

Will the murderer be punished for his crime? We shall see.

I have already spoken of my surprise to find the houses of slaveholders so generally destitute of books. Even wealthy men of this class, who can read themselves, are frequently found without more than half a dozen books in their families. In conversation upon this subject with a slaveholder, who was a native of New England, — a gentleman of fine talents and great learning, and for many years devoted to improvements in systems of education, — he confessed his astonishment at finding

21

so few literary men and so great a paucity of books in the South. He said he had been in every State in the Union, except California, on business that gave him an acquaintance with educated men — that he was well acquainted in Maine — and that he had no doubt there were more books, and more men of liberal education, and more business talent in the city of Portland, with its twenty-five thousand inhabitants, than in the whole State of Georgia, — and more in the State of Maine, with her half a million inhabitants, than in all the slave States! No gentleman in the country was better qualified to make the comparison, as he had no motive to make one unfavorable to the South, being identified with all its interests and institutions.

I visited the academy in the city of D., Georgia. Sixteen pupils only were present on examination day. Long seats, without backs or writing desks, and a small black-board, composed the whole inventory of accommodations, fixtures, and apparatus. This school was in operation only during the winter term.

While the teacher was demonstrating a sum on the board, two lads had a misunderstanding, and one of them knocked the other down. The noise attracted the attention of the teacher, who looked around before the boy had time to get up; but he took no notice of it. The recitations in reading and arithmetic — writing was inadmissible for want of writing desks — were far inferior to those in the common schools of New England.

I visited a school in M. county, where there were fourteen scholars, and only six books. The teacher was a native of that county, and the only native teacher in all the Oconee valley.

In the academy located in the county of L., I found a good teacher from New Hampshire. He assured me that he could not confine the boys at school long enough, without interruption, to teach them any thing thoroughly. "There," said he, pointing to a lad ten years of age, who appeared to be bright, "is a boy that has been here the most of a whole term,—but he has not learned all his letters. His father will permit no restraint upon him when he wishes for any amusement,—such as gaming and fishing,—and it is useless for me to try to teach him to read."

I spent the night with a slaveholder in one of the planting districts, and I inquired if he could read. He said he could not, nor could any of his family, except his son Henry. A Yankee schoolmaster had visited that place, and imposed upon the ignorant parents by assuring them that he could teach their children to read in a few days, on an improved method of teaching that art, for which he charged a high price, as it was "a great saving of time." Henry and several other boys in the place were sent to the Yankee's "patent" school, where they were simply taught to repeat two of Watts' hymns, while looking on the hymn book. This fact had previously come to my knowledge, and I remarked to the father that I would like to hear Henry read.

The old psalm book, the only book in the house, was brought out, and Henry opened at the right place, and read his two hymns. But I noticed the absence of the tone and emphasis peculiar to an intelligent reader. I opened at another place, and requested Henry to read there.

"I have not learned to read that hymn, sir," he replied.

His father was wealthy, owned much land, and large flocks and herds; but neither he, nor his wife, nor either of his six children, could read the alphabet.

A slaveholder in the interior, who owned forty slaves, and a large landed property, went to the market with ship timber. I purchased a raft of pine timber of him, and when I took a receipt for it, he made his mark. He had nine sons — all men grown — neither of whom could write his name. I said to the father, —

"Why in the world have you not expended a few thousand dollars of your property, to have your sons taught to read and write?"

The old gentleman had no idea that any advantage whatever was derived from such knowledge, except that it qualified its possessor to cheat his neighbor. For, said he, —

"I have always been cheated most by men who could write. Send my sons to school to learn to read and write? Not I! It would make just such devils of them as you Yankees are!

"I never make my mark, when I can help it," he added. "I bought a clock once of a man from Connecticut, warranted to *last* ninety-nine years. The price agreed upon was ten dollars. I had no money by me, and I gave the pedler an order on a merchant for that amount, as I supposed. But when the order came back, *forty* dollars were demanded of me. I refused to pay more than *ten*, and was sued. I went into court, and told the judge that the order was just *ten dollars*, and all my family were ready to swear to it. But the judge said that the *writing* was *forty;* and I, and all my boys couldn't swear a dollar off from that.

'Well judge,' said I, 'if there is so much deviltry in writing as that, I don't want my boys to learn to write. But look here, judge! there is a warrant the rascal gave me to keep the clock going. He was to pay back the ten dollars if it stopped in ninety-nine years, — and it stopped within a week.'

"The judge took the paper, and looked at it, and then laughed, as he read it aloud — '*warranted to last ninety-nine years.*' And all the lawyers laughed right smart. The judge then said to me,

'This *writing*, Capt. B., does not warrant the clock to *keep time*, but only to *last* ninety-nine years; — which means, I suppose, that if you keep your house well shingled, the clock will not *rot* during all that time.

"Now do you suppose I am fool enough, since that," said Capt. B., with a significant turn of the head, "to believe there is any benefit in learning to write?"

A description of the guide-posts, now in use in some districts of the South may be of some interest. There is a general trail through the woods, and across the old plantations, from one county seat to another, which enables the traveler to keep the right direction. But *mile-*

posts are erected, having as many notches cut in them as there are miles between each post and the next county seat. These posts are hard pine, hewn six inches square, and standing several feet out of the ground. Four grooves are cut *half* way across the post, for the first four numerals; then one *entirely* across for the fifth, — then four more half lines for the next four numbers, and another whole line for the tenth.

I was much amused while riding with a slaveholder in an old mule-cart one very dark, rainy evening, with his slave, "Pompey," for a driver. The master discovered the top of a mile-post, on a hill; and he told Pompey to jump out and see how far they were from home. Pompey alighted, and counted up, "one, two, three, four;" but when his finger reached the fifth groove, in tracing it out, he found it was no longer than either of the first four, and he was perplexed; for he had no idea of "*five*," except that it was twice as long as either of the other numerals.

As I returned the next day, I perceived what had bothered him. Some roguish boy had cut off the long end of the five, making it equal in length to all above and below it — as the distance was nine miles.

After fumbling over the notches awhile, and stuttering in loud whispers, with the rain pelting his bare head severely, he exclaimed, —

"Master, what devilish fool made this guide-post! No five here! All one, two, three, four — one, two three, four!"

Following the line of these guide-posts, I was dropped

down at a log-house tavern. After supper, I inquired of the landlord, whose father was from New England, if there was any thing going on in that village of a literary nature, to interest a stranger.

"Nothing, sir," said he, "except a singing school. We have a very good singing school this winter. They are singing now, right out there at the school house."

I started at once for the school house, wondering how music could be taught, where so many of the people could not read. When I arrived at the building, I saw it was an old, black, log house, built by the pioneers. There was a large opening in one end, too wide to be closed by a door; and as the music was in progress, and others were passing in, I mingled with the crowd, and entering in, took a stand in the corner. There was no light in the room except what came from the pitch-wood in the rock fireplace. There was no book in the school. All were taught by rote. Sixty pupils, three of whom were colored, were singing all on one part — the treble. Occasionally the colored boys — who have better ears, put in the harmony.

Soon as the choir came to a period, I said to the teacher that I hoped he would excuse my intrusion there, as I was fond of good music. He was very polite, and said that "no apology was necessary, as he was gratified to have me present." He seemed conscious of ability to teach music, and asked me if they did not sing well.

"Remarkably well," I replied, — for I was indeed surprised to hear them sing so well. "But do you not use books, sir, in teaching music?" I asked, with a little

"O, no, sir," he replied quickly, in a tone of decided prejudice against *book* knowledge. "We don't believe in this blind note-singing, here."

The next morning a member of that school, a young man twenty-two years of age, the son of a slaveholder, came to the tavern and desired me to inform him "what kind of a thing a singing book was," — assuring me that he had never seen one.

Ex-Governor Gilmer, of Georgia, in an address before the members of the legislature of that State, on the subject of temperance, is reported to have said —

"I hope the time is rapidly passing away, when the old may lead the young to dram shops; when daily fights between neighbors, in cups, make delightful amusement for the crowd; — and when members of the legislature cannot read the laws they help to pass!"

In the early history of our country, when books were scarce and expensive, our fathers were in the habit of singing at church without hymn books, — the minister reading aloud one line at a time, and then the congregation joining to sing it. Since the multiplication of books, this practice is discontinued. But it still prevails in the South. I noticed it in five different counties in Georgia. In such cases there are no books except the one used by the clergyman. And in one case, a Presbyterian minister, preaching in the city where I spent the Sabbath, finding no hymn book in the church, was obliged to wait until a boy went out to hunt one up.

About five thousand, of the nearly four hundred thousand slaves in Georgia, have been taught to read and write. These are generally owned by wealthy slaveholders, who have them taught in spite of the laws forbidding it, when it will better serve their own interest and convenience. It is a fine of thirty dollars and thirty-nine lashes to teach a slave to read in the city of Savannah. But wealthy slaveholders are above all law, except the conventional code of their own caste; and when they want servants to go to market to transact business, to pass letters and papers from family to family, they learn them to read names, and to write simple directions, and reckon small sums.

Sometimes also, the children of clergymen are encouraged to instruct young slaves, and it is winked at, — as an indulgence to the clerical office. But the *poor* slaveholders — and the mass are poor — never venture to learn their slaves to read. They are opposed to such instruction. And only a few slaves, therefore, — the favored house servants of the wealthy, — are taught to read. Though, occasionally, an intelligent slave, thirsting for knowledge, secretly learns the art without any assistance.

It is a fact often overlooked, that the free colored people of this country nearly all remain in the South. This is not because they have any privileges there which they prize, — but mainly on account of the climate. In the four States of Virginia, Georgia, and the two Carolinas, in 1850 the free colored population was 93,000. If any Northern men have feared that the slaves, in case of emancipation, would emigrate in large numbers to the free States, a glance at the census tables will show them how groundless are their fears. The slaves, if set free, will always be wanted in the South. All the difference emancipation will make, will be the restoration of their rights, and free, voluntary labor, for a just compensation, instead of compulsory, unpaid toil. The fact that the great body of free colored men now prefer to live in the South, where they are denied all rights as citizens, — where it is a criminal offense to teach them the alphabet, is sufficient proof that the South is their natural home. My present inquiry, however, is how far this large class of the population of this country enjoy the blessings of education. In this respect the laws of the slave States rank them with the slaves. All instruction is forbidden under heavy penalties.

I have frequently alluded to the fact that slavery, in Virginia, is divested of many of its harshest features. In that State there is a free colored population of some sixty thousand. The Governor has for several years gravely recommended that they all be driven from the State! This inhuman and barbarous scheme has been discussed in the legislature, but has so far failed. Still, in Virginia, as in other slave States, the laws prohibit any instruction of these persons. The following narrative will show the state of public opinion there, and in the light of it we may see the condition of the free colored population of the South.

About two years ago, a Mrs. Douglas, of Norfolk, and her daughter, were arrested, and she was imprisoned in that city, for teaching colored children to read. After she had suffered the penalty provided by law, and was set at liberty, she published a little volume, giving an account of the circumstances. Her story is one of much interest. She is a native of the South, having been born in the city of Washington. She states that in 1845 she removed to Norfolk, where, with an only daughter, she lived a quiet and unobtrusive life, until Dec., 1853. She supported herself and child by vest making, and was at last induced, by the force of circumstances, to engage in the religious and moral instruction of a few free colored children. Her first pupils were three girls and two boys, the children of a barber, all of whose family were free. The circumstances of the arrest are thus stated:

"All was going on as peaceable as usual, and I had taken my seat to commence my daily toil, when a loud knock was made at my front door. I answered it myself, when the face of an officer presented itself, who inquired who lived up stairs. I replied that I alone occupied the house. He then asked if Mrs. Douglas lived there. I told him that I was Mrs. Douglas.

He said, "You keep a school?"

"Yes, sir," was my reply.

"A school for colored children?"

I answered, "yes."

"I must see those children," said he.

I then demanded what business he had with them, or anything in my house. He replied, that he had been sent by the mayor.

"Very good," said I; "walk in, and you shall see them." And, without giving my daughter or the children any notice, I invited him up into the school room. Never will I forget the frightened state of those children, and the countenance of their young teacher. My daughter sat paralyzed, covering her face with her hands; and it was some time before I could restore order in the room. Some were crying, some exclaiming, "Oh my! oh my!" and some clinging around me in their terror; but during the excitement I never lost my presence of mind.

As soon as I had restored quiet in the room, I inquired of Mr. Cherry, the city constable, what he wanted with those children. He replied that he must take them before the mayor.

"Very well," said I, "my daughter and myself will accompany them."

To my astonishment, he went to the head of the stairs and gave a loud rap with his club, when another officer made his appearance, entering from the back door. For a moment I thought my house was surrouuded by officers, who perhaps fancied they had found a nest of thieves. They then noted down the names of all the children, as well as those of their parents. When they had finished, I politely informed Mr. Cherry that they were all free children, and all, or nearly all, members of the Christ's Church Sunday School.

"It makes no difference, madam," replied he; "it is a violation of the law to teach any person of color to read or write, slave or free; and an act punishable by imprisonment in the penitentiary."

"Very well," I replied, "if they send me to the penitentiary, it will be in a good cause, and not a disgraceful one."

"Even this information, which was the most profound news to me, did not unnerve me at all; for I remembered that our Savior was persecuted for doing good, and why should I not be? This thought strengthened me to bear my own persecution for ten long months afterwards."

XX.

SLAVERY AND THE SABBATH.

"Oh! welcome to the wearied Earth
The Sabbath resting comes,
Gathering the sons of toil and care
Back to their peaceful homes;
And, like a portal to the skies,
Opens the House of God,
Where all who seek may come and learn
The way the Savior trod."

MRS. HALE.

ONE of the strangest sights to a New England man, on visiting the Southern States, is the desecration of the Sabbath. In some of the cities, especially if a good number of the business men are from the North, the churches are tolerably well attended, — there being but one service for the day. But even here the afternoon and evening are much devoted to amusements. And, in fact, throughout the entire South, with not very numerous exceptions, the Sabbath, instead of being a day of rest, or of worship, is a holiday — occupied mainly in pleasure and sport.

The first sounds that salute the ear, not only in the country, but in many of the cities of the South, on Sabbath morning, are the firing of guns, the beating of drums, and the noise of the hunting horn. They have boat parties, riding parties, hunting parties, fishing parties, drinking parties, gaming parties, and dancing parties. And the Sabbath is almost invariably the day for horse races, and military parades. A colporteur of the American Tract Society, writing to the Maine *Christian Mirror*, under date of May 9, 1854, says —

"In Mississippi, where I am laboring, drinking, gaming, and horse racing are common on the Sabbath — and the Sabbath is distinguished from other days by the firing of guns."

There is more travel in the South on the Sabbath, than on any other day of the week. To ascertain this fact I examined the registers at the boat offices, hotels, and public boarding houses; and I uniformly found that a larger number of names was entered by travelers on the Sabbath than on any other day. The Sabbath is spent by travelers not only in visiting friends, but in traveling long distances on business. The passenger trains on the railroads run for this purpose. The boats on the rivers are employed in this service. And clergymen, except when their duties confine them at home, are quite as likely to travel on the Sabbath as others. I was told by a delegate from a New England Conference to the Presbyterian General Assembly, that a large part of the Southern ministers who were there, traveled on the Sabbath before that body convened.

Sabbath evening in the South is a time of unusual dissipation. Theaters and other like places of amusement are open, and thronged more than any other evening;

while the drinking saloons, billiard rooms, and other dens of infamy, are frequented by the riotous and noisy crowd.

A large majority of the slaves labor on the Sabbath, almost from necessity. In some of the cities most of them rest; but in the planting districts many of them labor more or less — not usually at the daily task — but they wash and iron, make and mend their garments, cut wood, and work in their gardens.

But the slaves do not labor for themselves alone. In the planting districts, especially during the busy season of the year, the slaves are not permitted to make the Sabbath even a holiday. Instances are by no means rare, even among masters professing to be Christians, in which the slaves are compelled to labor on the Sabbath as on other days.

Rev. H. B. Abbott, pastor of the M. E. Church at Augusta, Me., was formerly a counselor at law in Mississippi. In a letter to me dated April 10, 1854, he says —

"I am acquainted with a Baptist preacher in Mississippi who compelled his slaves to labor on the Sabbath, and justified himself under the plea that, if they were not at work, they would be sporting, and roving about the fields and woods, thereby desecrating the Sabbath more than by laboring under an overseer."

I was spending a Sabbath in the city of A. Early in the day I noticed the planters from the surrounding country, coming in to attend the morning service. Many of them were members of the city churches. They remained in the city after the meetings were closed, and about noon, or a little later, their slaves began to arrive, with mule teams, loaded with cotton, and other kinds of produce. In the afternoon the stores were opened, and these Christian slaveholders exchanged their produce for groceries, and other commodities, with which they sent their slaves home, while they remained, drinking whisky and cracking jokes, until the cool of the evening.

The Sabbath before the State election, is denominated "*free liquor day*," in Georgia, — a strange title for that day, in a Christian land. It is so called, from the custom of those who are candidates for office to invite all who propose to vote for them to their "head quarters," on that day, to partake of spirituous liquors at their expense.

In the old city of Augusta, Georgia, it seemed more like home to me on the Sabbath, than at any place I visited in the South. The people generally attended church, and refrained from labor, and from amusements.

At Savannah the Independent Presbyterian church was well filled. The Episcopal church also, in that city, had no vacant seats. But few were present at the Presbyterian and Unitarian churches. In the latter, Rev. Mr. Pierpont, the pastor, was honored with only forty-two auditors, on a pleasant Sabbath. I heard a clergyman state at a temperance meeting in Savannah, that there were fourteen hundred members of evangelical churches in that city, and the average attendance upon divine worship was not more than sixteen hundred. The free population was about fifteen thousand. One reason he gave for this, was, that many of the people were accustomed to be intoxicated Saturday night, and therefore, were unable to attend church on the Sabbath.

A respectable number were present at some of the churches in Macon, Lagrange, and other places where schools are kept in operation. But in the planting districts,—where nine-tenths of the white population reside,—there is seldom a congregation of more than fifty persons collected in a church, and these are few and far between.

I passed a beautiful Christmas Sabbath at Albany, the county seat of Baker county. This city contains some twenty stores, and exports annually about 12,000 bales of cotton. The Baptist clergyman was sick,—the Presbyterian clergyman had gone away discouraged,—and the Methodist church was the only one opened on that day. Thirty-nine persons only were present at that church, three of whom were colored. There were three thousand souls within sound of a church-going bell, had there been one. Where were they?

At Oglethorpe, a smart young city at the termination of the South-western railroad, where there was a population of over three thousand, there was no church service during the Sabbath I spent there.

At Dublin, an old city, Rev. Mr. Parsons, Presbyterian, preached to a congregation of forty-eight,—two of whom were slaves,—on a pleasant Sabbath. There was no other church in that city. The population was two thousand.

All over the planting districts, as I have before said, very few attend church, and very few of the churches have constant preaching. There was not a settled minister of the gospel, of any denomination, who preached constantly at the same place, for more than two hundred miles, on the stage road leading from the coast to the capital; and yet, in each of those counties, from six to thirteen churches are returned in the census. Traveling ministers preach at several different stations, and the number of sermons delivered at each church will not average more than one a month.

A colporteur of the American Tract Society, in 1854, reports of one of the counties of North Carolina, that "*three-fourths* of the people are destitute of public services on the Sabbath; and that about *one-third* of the parents can read and write, cast accounts, and guage a barrel of brandy."

Another says, "I visited 60 families, numbering 221 souls over ten years of age; only 23 could read, and 17 write; 41 were destitute of the Bible; the average of their going to church was once in 7 years. Several between 30 and 45 years old had heard but one or two sermons in their lives. Some grown up youths had never heard a sermon or a prayer until my visit, and did not know of such a being as a Savior; and girls and boys from ten to fifteen did not know who made them. All of one family rushed away when I knelt to pray, to a neighbor's, begging them to tell what I meant by it."

I have already given a brief description of the churches in the planting districts of the South. Like the abodes of the planters, they are rough, and rude, throughout. They are often made of logs, are destitute of windows, without pews, or pulpits. Instead of these, there are rough seats, without backs or benches, where the preacher and the "crowd" sit together on a common level. These rude buildings are not kept sacred as temples of worship. The wild, uncultivated habits of the people are inconsistent with such an idea. Hence the church is free for any other exercise, or for any kind of amusements.

I attended church in M—— county, one Sabbath, where more than half the young men who came to attend the meeting, remained out of doors. They kept passing in and out in little squads of two or three at a time, and very little attention was paid to the services. It was a log church, with no windows, and only one narrow door, which was kept open; and from my seat I noticed some young men drinking on the outside. A little distance beyond were some gaming tables,—and further out into the woods they were trotting horses.

In another county I attended church where both the house and the people were equally coarse and repulsive. Being invited, with the clergyman, after the close of service, to pass the evening and night in the family of a Christian slaveholder, I accepted the invitation. I had previously been informed by the clergyman that our host, Mr. D., was one of the best men in the world,—always looking up objects of charity,—giving bread to the hungry, bestowing kind attentions upon the sick, the bereaved, and the distressed.

Mr. D. was one of three members, in a church of forty, who had embraced temperance principles. He had heartily espoused the cause, was fully convinced that total abstinence was the only remedy for intemperance, and nothing could induce him to take a drop of any thing containing alcohol, unless he believed it absolutely necessary for his health. I had previously addressed a temperance meeting in that place, and Mr. D. had expressed much gratitude for the apparently good impression made, and a hope that it might influence church members, at least, to become sober men.

Mr. D. owned a large real estate, numerous flocks, and herds, and swine, all roaming at large in the forests. He and his excellent wife were about fifty years of age. They had both sons and daughters of age, and they owned one slave girl — Nelly — a bright, smart quadroon. But Mrs. D. and her daughters worked in the kitchen with Nelly, and the sons labored with Mr. D. on the farm.

When we arrived at their house, after the morning exercises at the church, I noticed that the sons and daughters did not come home; and I asked the father where his children were.

"O, they have stopped at the meeting house, I suppose," replied he.

"For what purpose?" I asked. "There is no meeting this afternoon."

"I know that," said he; "but the young folks always stop to have a talk, or a frolic, after meeting is out."

"What kind of a frolic?"

"Why, they sometimes dance, and sing, and do anything they please."

"I want to know, Mr. D.," said I, "if you have dancing in your church on the Sabbath?"

"Oh, yes," he answered, sadly, "and we always shall have, as long as church members drink whisky."

"Do you know of any other church, Mr. D., where they have such amusements on the Sabbath?"

"I know of none where they do not," he answered.

"Do you know this because you have seen it? Or have you only heard it was so?"

"Well," said he, "I will tell you what I lately saw myself. I was down to the county seat at the last court. We had a murder case there from this neighborhood, and nearly all the people went down, some on foot, some on horseback. We started to come home Saturday evening, and just as we came to the Methodist church, about dark, a terrible thunder shower came down upon us. One of them, a lawyer, said we had better go into the meeting-house, and stay all night, as there was no other house near the church. Soon after we entered the church, they sent a nigger off after a fiddler, and some whisky. When the fiddler and the whisky came, I told the lawyer — the only man who had a watch — that I would thank him to let me know when midnight had come. He did so; and I went out into the woods and lay there until daylight. I had little sleep, for the noise and dancing in the church kept me awake; but I would not stay in the House of God, when there was drinking and dancing there on the Sabbath day."

After I had secured the confidence of Mr. D., as he certainly had secured mine, I informed him that I was as much opposed to slavery as he possibly could be to intemperance; that it was no part of my mission in that place to talk, as I had done, on the subject of temperance; but that I was traveling to obtain facts in relation to the treatment of slaves, and the effects of slavery on the masters and their families, and upon the interests and institutions of the South.

"What good do you think that will do *you*?" he asked.

"It will enable me to inform the people of the North what slavery is," I replied; "for we wish to have it abolished."

"What for?" he inquired, with a look and tone indicating great surprise, as if he knew not what it meant.

"Can you read, Mr. D.?" I inquired.

"No, sir."

"Can Mrs. D. read?"

"She cannot. None of my family can read, except Henry."

These inquiries may seem abrupt and impertinent to Northern minds; but such questions are often asked in the South. And it is truly astonishing that such men as Mr. D., who had the means to educate himself and family, should neglect it.

"Don't your ministers say anything about slavery, in the pulpit, Mr. D.?" I asked.

"Not very often," he replied. "I never heard any of them say anything against it."

"Have you never heard a minister say it was wrong?"

"I have heard them say it was wicked to *abuse* the slaves, — but nothing more."

"Have you never heard a minister say that the slaves ought to have their liberty?"

"I never have, sir! Why should the ministers say the niggers ought to be free, when most of them own some themselves?"

"You own one slave, do you not, Mr. D.?"

"Yes! I have one here — Nelly — that you have seen come in from the kitchen."

"May I ask you, then," said I, "if you have ever thought whether it was *wrong* for you to hold that girl as a slave?"

"No! If I thought it was wrong, I would give her her liberty at once."

"Why did not Nelly go to meeting? And why don't she come in to prayers? I notice all your children do," I remarked.

"We don't think it of much consequence for niggers to go to meeting," he replied.

"Why not?" I asked.

"Why not? Because the ministers say there is some doubt about niggers having souls!"

"*No souls!*" I exclaimed. "Why! What kind of beings do you think they are, Mr. D.?"

"Oh, I have heard folks say they are a kind of creature between men and monkies, connecting men with other animals."

Nelly, I have said, was a quadroon, — a bright, sensible girl of seventeen. She possessed more knowledge, and had, apparently, more good common sense than the whole family of her new master.

"Where did you get that slave, Mr. D.?"

"I bought her out of a drove."

"How long have you owned her?"

"Four years."

"Where was she raised?"

"She came from Virginia, I believe," he replied.

"Do you know who was her former owner?"

"I do not, exactly; but I heard her say, when I first bought her, that her mother told her he was a minister."

"Was she living with her mother?"

"Yes, I believe she was."

"Do you know whether she had a father, or any brothers and sisters, living at that time?"

"No, sir," he replied; "we never ask these niggers anything about their folks."

I had previously learned that purchasers of slaves seldom, if ever, inquire of them whether they have left friends behind them. It would keep alive sympathies in the heart of the slave that the masters wish to smother.

Hence I asked the question. And it did not surprise me that neither Mr. D., nor his wife, nor either of his daughters had ever inquired of Nelly, during the four years she had resided in the family, whether she had any relatives living.

"Are you willing, Mr. D.," said I, "to have Nelly called in, and let me inquire of her about her friends in Virginia?"

He did not wait to answer me, but stepped to the door and called the girl, who was at work in the kitchen, about forty yards from the house. Nelly ran through the yard, and entering the house, inquired what her master wanted.

"Here is a friend of mine from the North, Nelly," said Mr. D., "who wants to talk with you about your folks up in Virginia."

I can assure the reader that Nelly appeared entirely free from embarrassment in the presence of her master. She knew him to be an upright, truthful man, — that what he promised he would perform, — and she believed and trusted him.

"Will you tell me, Nelly," said I, "where you were raised?"

She darted towards Mr. D., and whispered anxiously, "Does the gentleman wish to buy me, master?"

"Oh no, Nelly," replied the master. "I will not sell you to anybody as long as I live."

"No, no, Nelly!" said I. "You need not be afraid of that; for I wouldn't take you as a gift, unless your master wanted to send you to the North, where you could be free."

"Well, I don't want to go anywhere to be free!"

"So I suppose, Nelly. But we have no slaves where I live. I don't want to buy you, nor take you away. I am your friend, and only asked your master to call you in, that I might ask you about the slaves where you was raised."

"Very well, master," she replied.

"Where was you raised, Nelly?"

"I was born in Richmond; but our family moved out into a place in the country, on James river."

"Was your master a minister?"

"Yes, sir."

"How do you know that? Did you go to meeting?"

"No, sir! But my mother told me he was a minister; and besides, I used to put his books in place, and clean up his room when he was gone to church."

"Then you had a mother living?"

"Oh, yes, sir! My mother was living when I was sold."

"And was your father living, Nelly?"

"Yes, sir! My father was alive too, and I had one little brother, and ——"

Here she paused, as if struck with the thought that she was exceeding the bounds of her liberty, by speaking of a brother or sisters before she was inquired of respecting them.

"One brother, you say, Nelly; and how many sisters?"

"I had five sisters, master; and one little brother, just beginning to run about the kitchen, and to speak little words."

"Were any of them sold before you, Nelly?"

"No, sir! I was the *first* one that had to be sold."

"How came you to be sold?"

"Well,—just before I was sold, my mistress died, and master had his rooms dressed in mourning. He had crape hung all around in the parlor, and the sitting-room, and even in his study; and when the merchant sent in the bill for the crape, my mother told me" ——

Here the words choked her utterance. The word *mother* revived in her memory the old home affections, the family sympathies, the instinctive attachments, — strongest in the African race, — and they all came thronging back upon her mind, and she could not speak.

"Why don't you tell him, and be done with it?" said her master, not seeming to comprehend the load of anguish that was crushing her heart. After waiting until a flood of tears had brought a little relief, she continued —

"My mother told me — that — the merchant's bill — for the crape — was several hundred dollars, — and — that I — *was sold to pay it!*"

And she sank down on the floor, as exhausted, and helpless as though she had been stricken down with paralysis! Her master went to the back part of the room, sat down, and wept like a child!!

XXI.

SLAVERY AND CHRISTIANITY.

"The theme divine at cards she'll not forget,
But takes in texts of scripture at piquet;
In those licentious meetings acts the prude,
And thanks her Maker that her cards are good."

YOUNG.

THE type of morality, in any country, is seldom much higher in the church than it is in respectable society out of it. It is not within the range of my design to explain this, — though, to my mind, it shows the great influence and the corresponding responsibility of the churches. In no civilized countries do men of good standing in society justify themselves in any practices which are not countenanced by professors of Christianity. This was true in the most corrupt days of the Romish Church. It is no less true now. It was, therefore, no mere rhetorical flourish, but the utterance of a great truth, founded in the nature of man, and based on the power of the Christian faith, when Rev. Albert Barnes declared that slavery could not live an hour out of the church, if it were not sustained within it.

With this principle in view, we may know, without visiting the South, how the Christian churches have been corrupted. We need not expect to find a higher standard of morality within, than without. If men of high social position out of the church own slaves, so will church members. And so is the fact. There are more than six hundred thousand slaves held in bondage in the South by men professing to be Christians. Is it a common practice in the South, among respectable men, to visit theaters and horse-races on the Sabbath, — to drink intoxicating liquors to excess, — to play cards, and gamble, — to make the Sabbath a day of sport and pleasure seeking? These practices obtain as well in the churches, as out of them. And just as a slaveholder who is known to own, and buy, and sell his own children as slaves, suffers nothing at all in his reputation on that account,—so, if such a slaveholder belongs to the church, these facts do not affect his standing there. The thing is so common throughout the South, — among men calling themselves Christians, as well as others, — as hardly to attract attention.

I have already alluded to the alarming extent to which intemperance prevails in the South. There are some noble men there, who see this evil, and are using all the influence in their power to provide a proper remedy. But not in our day can we hope for the Maine Law to triumph in the slave States.

Some of the clergymen in Georgia are true temperance men, and they are persecuted as bitterly as were the early anti-slavery ministers in New England. Hence they seldom speak of the subject except at temperance meetings, and there cautiously and timidly. The churches will not tolerate it in the pulpit.

I was pleased to hear Mr. K., one of the speakers in a temperance meeting at Savannah, — a gentleman who was afterwards President of the Georgia State Temperance Convention, — speak of the Constitution of the United States in a manner that showed his manly independence. Slaveholders are not afraid to speak! There are no cringing doughfaces in the South. And no men more heartily despise such creatures than do the slaveholders, — even when using them for their purposes.

"We are told," said Mr. K., "that the Constitution of these States so guarantees and guards the commerce of the country that it legalizes the trade in spirits; and that a law prohibiting the sale of intoxicating drinks would be unconstitutional. If such be the fact, let the people get together again and amend it. Or if we find it cannot be amended so as to stop rumselling, let us *tear it in pieces, and make a new and better one!*"

In the city of Savannah the slaves are allowed a free indulgence in the use of wine at the communion table, as an inducement, probably, for them to enter the church, and to make them better contented with their condition as slaves. A gentleman of the first respectability, residing in that city, informed me that he saw a ten gallon demijohn filled with wine in a store on Sabbath morning, and he followed the man who took it to the colored church, where there was a meeting of the colored churches for the communion. And he said that they drank nearly the whole of it.

"Did they drink more," I asked, "than is generally used for that purpose by other churches?"

"O yes," he replied. "I never saw such drinking wine in my life!"

The number that partook at that time was estimated to be about eighty, which would afford them about a pint each.

It is worthy of remark that this is the church where the author of the "*South Side View of Slavery*" saw such remarkable evidences of piety while he was worshipping there. And the old slave preacher, the pastor of that church, to whom Dr. Adams alludes, is notoriously dishonest, as I was informed by a merchant of that city. But he succeeded so well in preaching, that a few prayerless slaveholders aided him to purchase some slaves — three in number, I believe — so that he might be able to give, in his own person, an example of a slaveholding minister of the gospel preaching that gospel to his own race!

The subject of intemperance in the colored churches was a topic of conversation in a store at Darien; and I stated some facts which had come to my knowledge, showing the intemperate habits of members in those churches in the cities. And I freely expressed my opinion, that slaveholders encouraged their slaves to unite with the churches mainly to enhance their market value. A clergyman present, who participated in the discussion, attempted to defend these churches.

"You must have been misinformed," said he; "for I know the slaves to be as good christians as the masters who are members of churches."

"I have no desire to draw a comparison between the slaves and their masters," I replied; "but I believe, of course, what I have seen myself."

There was in that store a gentleman formerly from Brooklyn, N. Y., where, for several years, he attended the ministry of Rev. H. W. Beecher. He was a firm friend of free principles, and he exhibited an independence of thought and speech in maintaining them. He was at that time connected with a business firm in that city.

"You are correctly informed, sir," said he, addressing himself to me. "This business of getting slaves into the church is all a humbug. And now I will tell you what took place here last autumn.

"The overseer from Butler's Island," — on which there are several hundred slaves, on a beautiful rice plantation, out in the arms of the Altamaha, all in sight, and within fifty rods of the store in which we stood, — "came over here one Saturday night, and inquired of a minister if he would baptize some slaves belonging to that island the next day. The clergyman replied that he would, if they seemed to be worthy subjects of baptism. Sabbath afternoon, a large number of the slaves came down to the bank of the river. The preacher asked those who were proposed for baptism a few questions, such as, whether they believed in a God? a state of future happiness and misery? the necessity of repentance and faith? to every one of which they all answered, 'yes, master,' 'yes, master.' Not a question was put to them that required a negative answer. The ordinance had been administered to about forty, when the minister said the waters were so cold, and he was so tired, that they would adjourn to the next day. Monday afternoon the exercises were resumed, and the solemn ceremonies went on until some seventy-five were baptized.

"Now I have never heard that a gospel sermon was ever preached on Butler's Island. I have been all over it, and I never saw a Bible there. Those slaves had, evidently, no more idea of the solemn obligations they were taking upon them in making a religious profession than the brutes. And as proof of this, after the solemn farce was ended some of those slaves who had been baptized came over here and staid a long time that afternoon, drinking whisky to intoxication. One of them absolutely stole a bundle of wet clothes that a brother had just been baptized in. I saw him, detected him, challenged him with it, and he confessed it! And yet I think an account of this baptism was published in some Northern papers as *a great revival of religion on Butler's Island!*"

The colored churches in the South, of course, have no *pastors*, in any proper sense of that term. Sometimes the pastor of the church to which their masters belong condescends to address them. But their meetings, if they have any speaker at all, are usually addressed by colored preachers. The tenor of their sermons has been so often described, that I will not repeat any of them. If these preachers are honest, they counsel obedience and submission, because otherwise they would not be permitted to speak. If they are dishonest, as some of them are, they preach to please the masters, just as time-serving ministers do in the North.

Dr. Nelson — author of the able work on infidelity published by the American Tract Society — after a residence of more than forty years in North Carolina, and an intimate acquaintance with slavery, says,

"I say what I know when I speak in relation to this matter. I have been intimately acquainted with the religious opportunities of the slaves, — in the constant habit of hearing the sermons which are preached to them. And I solemnly affirm that, during the forty years of my residence and observation in this line, I never heard a single one of these sermons but what was taken up with the obligations and duties of slaves to their masters. Indeed, I never heard a sermon to slaves but what made obedience to masters by the slaves the fundamental and supreme law of religion. Any candid and intelligent man can decide whether such preaching is not, as to religious purposes, worse than none at all."

It is not strange, therefore, that the slaves are degraded. The Synod of South Carolina and Georgia only declared what was the natural, inevitable result of the slave system, when they said that the slaves were "in the condition of heathen, — and in some respects, a worse condition. Their moral and religious condition is such, that they may justly be considered the *heathen of this Christian country!*"

And yet I should be doing the slaves injustice to deny that there are many sincere Christians among them. With all their darkness and ignorance, there are doubtless many devout worshipers, living up to the dim light they have. I became acquainted with many such, who, like "Uncle Tom," and "Aunt Chloe," while they suffer all things for Christ's sake here, and seem to us so benighted, in the sight of Him who looketh on the heart, are, it may be, far in advance of many Christians who now assume to look down on them with as much of contempt as of pity. Many of us, perhaps, who think we are first shall be last, and the last shall be first.

I have just read, with much interest, a letter from a lady who is spending the present summer (1855) in the South, published in the *Hartford Republican.*

"I have just been to visit a plantation, 'Botten Garden' is the name of it. The owner is a very rich man and resides in the town. His plantation consists of sixteen hundred acres of black prairie land. Six hundred acres were in cotton in one field, and three hundred in corn. The fields look beautifully at this season of the year. Not a weed is to be seen, and the rows are very straight and extend as far as the eye can reach. Mr. R. let the slaves leave their work for the remainder of the day, that we might see them together. I should think there were fifty children too young to work at all, playing in the yard. I called them all together and they sung for me; — *all* sing. They took hold of hands, forming a circle, and went round a tree, singing, 'I'm gwine away up yonder,' 'See God, feedin on de lambs!' and 'When I get ober Jordan, I'll be a hero den.'

"I asked the women to sing. There has been a great revival on the plantation, and all are very pious. They sing nothing but hymns. They sung a very long hymn. This was the chorus: 'Oh sister, watch dat heart, dat 'ceitful, 'ceitful heart, for I'm gwine home.' I could hardly keep back the tears, they seemed so solemn, and looked up so earnestly in my face. I went round to their houses alone and made calls. They all talked constantly upon religion, and I could not get in a word. Indeed I had rather listen, for I *knew* that the Spirit takes of the things of Jesus, and shows it unto them, and the way of salvation is made clear to them in this way, though they are denied the privilege of reading God's blessed word.

"I know but little of the horrors of slavery. *I see but the best side*, and that is none too good. Some slaves are just as white as I am. The other day I met a little slave girl. She certainly was the most beautiful child I ever saw. She was wading in a muddy creek and as I passed by, she looked up through her beautiful brown curls and said, 'I love the beautiful fishes.' I want to buy her, and make her a free and noble woman. I told a gentleman so. He said she could not be bought. It seems dreadful that one so beautiful should be so degraded. And *what* a life is before *her!* Her beauty will only make her more miserable. I cannot bear to think of it."

Slavery is inherently in direct antagonism to Christianity, —not only in matters of practice, but of doctrine. In its very nature it denies the authority of God to command the obedience and the worship of his creatures. The slave must, *at his peril*, obey his master in all things. Deny the master this claim, and you strike at the very foundation of the system. The slave has no power to protect or provide for his family. If his wife is sold away, he must cohabit with a stranger, to raise up children for the market.* God requires him to remember the Sabbath day, to keep it holy. But the master claims the right, and often exercises it, to abrogate God's law, and compel him to labor on the Sabbath. Slavery, therefore, not only denies the inalienable rights of man, — but it usurps the place of the Creator, and denies to the Almighty the right to rule over his creatures! And yet, religious bodies that have always had as keen a scent for heresy as the bloodhound has for his victim, have not yet found out whether it is heretical to deny the supremacy of God, and the manhood of those whom He has created in his own image!

"A few days since," says a late writer in the Boston *Congregationalist*, "a most affecting fact was stated to

---

* The Savannah River Baptist Association, in reply to the question, "Whether, in a case of involuntary separation, of such a character as to preclude all prospect of future intercourse, the parties ought to be allowed to marry again?" returned the following answer: "That such separation among persons situated as our slaves are, is *civilly* a separation by *death*, and they believe that, in the sight of God, it would be so viewed. To forbid second marriages in such cases, would be to expose the parties, not only to stronger hardships and strong temptation, but to church censure, for acting in obedience to their masters, who cannot be expected to acquiesce in a regulation at variance with justice to the slaves, and to the spirit of that command which regulates marriage among Christians. *The slaves are not free agents*, and a dissolution by death is not more entirely without their consent, and beyond their control, than by such separation."

us by the Rev. Mr. Alvord. During a residence of several months in Florida, for his health, he was often wont to take exercise by working with the slaves on the plantation where he was; and having gained their confidence thus, they freely opened their hearts to him as a friend, — a thing which slaves do not do to every man, and especially to chance visitors, whom they judge to be in the interest of their masters.

"In one case he called to see a slave who was in confinement for endeavoring to follow his conscience, in keeping holy the Sabbath day in the worship of God. By working nights, he actually performed the labor assigned for seven days, and then spent the Sabbath in worship. His master discovered it, and imprisoned him, and cut and mangled his body with scourges, to subdue his will, and compel him to work on the Sabbath. After the wounds began to heal, he cut them open from time to time by repeated scourgings. Mr. Alvord saw his wounds, and gazed with painful sympathy upon his honest face, wet with tears, as he told the severity of his trial. At last, after repeated scourgings, his spirit failed, and he submitted to his master's impious will."

Church discipline is almost unknown in the Southern churches, especially for anything relating to slaves. No matter how cruelly a master treats his servants, or how severely he punishes them — even unto death; if he does not violate the law — which it is hardly possible for him to do — the church will not censure him. I could relate many facts illustrating this subject, but one or two incidents will be sufficient.

The following story was related to me by Mr. D., the owner of Nelly, of whom I have given some account in the preceding chapter.

Mr. D. had a neighbor,—a member of the same church,—by the name of M. He was a wealthy, though an ignorant man, owning many slaves; and besides a plantation, with cattle, and mules, and sheep, he owned mills in that neighborhood. Among his slaves there was a house servant by the name of Nancy. One evening her master told her to go up to Mr. D.'s on some errand. It was a bright moonlight evening, but Nancy was afraid to go. Mr. D.'s son, Henry, had been bitten by a rattlesnake, though the wound was not fatal. He had not fully recovered when I was there. These snakes are supposed to be out in the moonlight evenings, and as they cannot be seen so distinctly as in the day time, they are the more dreaded. Under these circumstances, Nancy's fears were not strange. She therefore told her master that she was afraid to go. But he was enraged at her unwillingness to obey, and he commanded her to start at once. She still refused to go saying that the snakes would kill her, and that she would rather be whipped to death than go.

Mr. M. then commenced whipping her and he applied the lash again and again, until he saw that it was in vain. He was filled with rage, and taking a quart dish, he filled it full of filthy liquid from the barn yard, and put it to her lips; and after compelling her to drink a part of it, he asked her if she would then go.

"No, master; I will *die* first! I cannot go. I know the snakes will kill me if I go!"

And he whipped her until he made her drink it all. The next morning the poor girl was dead!

"Did you see the body after her death, Mr. D.?" I asked him.

"Yes, I went down to see her, and I never saw such a sight!"

"Was Nancy a Christian, Mr. D.?"

"She was a right good girl," he replied, with a deep sigh; and he added, *"She was a member of our church!"*

"Did your church discipline your brother M. for killing her?"

"Discipline! What do you mean by *that?"* inquired Mr. D., not knowing the meaning of the word.

"Did you call him to account?"

"Oh no! How could we? *He had not violated the law."*

I became acquainted with a young lady from Maine, who had been teaching school in the South a few years. She belongs to a family of the highest respectability in the city of ——, and at the time of her first going South, none of the family had any sympathy with the anti-slavery movement. The following incident was related to me by her, all the facts being within her own personal knowledge.

Mrs. C., — where this teacher was boarding, — owned a mulatto girl named "Chloe," who was expecting soon to be married to a slave boy named "Jok," who lived about five miles distant. I ought, perhaps, to have mentioned before this, that slaves, no matter how old, are always *boys* and *girls*. They never become *men* or *women*.

Jok went to his master on Saturday night, to obtain a pass to visit Chloe. His master was intoxicated, and therefore he could not write a pass. No other person in the neighborhood could write; and Jok's mistress told him it would not be safe for him to go without a pass, as it was contrary to law. Jok waited until morning. Chloe sat up all night, watching for him with deep anxiety, lest some evil had befallen him, fearing that he had been whipped, or sold away. Slaves are very faithful in fulfilling promises to visit friends, in order to remove such fears.

In the morning Jok's mistress told him that his master was still sick, and not able to write; but that he had been up to Mrs. C.'s so many times, she would run the risk to let him go without a pass.

"You tell Mrs. C.," said she, "that your master is sick, and that I sent you up there without a pass; and she will excuse it."

When Jok came up to the gate, the overseer went out, as his custom was, and demanded his pass. The slave informed him that his master was so sick he could not write one, that he waited all night for it, and his mistress told him to come without one.

"Go home, you scoundrel!" said the overseer, "and get your pass!"

Jok started back towards his home. Chloe, who had overheard the conversation, ran into the room of her mistress, and informed her that the overseer had driven Jok home after his pass, and she supposed, as it was early in the morning, that he came away before breakfast. Mrs. C. stepped to the back door and called Jim, — a young slave boy belonging to her, — and told him to run and overtake Jok and tell him to come back and see her before he went home to get his pass; not intending to countermand the order of the overseer. Jim ran to bring back Jok. In the meantime, the overseer went out to the stable. Just as the boys returned to the gate, he came in from the stable, and demanded of Jok again "why he was there without a pass?"

"Mrs. C. sent for me to come back," answered Jok.

"I don't care if she did," said the overseer; "you shan't go in."

"I tell you I must," urged Jok.

"Not a step!" forbade the overseer.

Now what should the poor boy do? Two slaveholders, equal in authority, commanding him to go in opposite directions. He thought he would press his way through the gate, by the overseer, and run to the door and ascertain what Mrs. C. wanted, and then go home for his pass. In attempting to do this, the overseer clinched him; but Jok proved to be the stronger man, and he threw him down. The overseer tried to choke him and strike him in the face. Mrs. C. ran out, and taking hold of Jok's arm, she exclaimed,

"Why, Jok, you don't know what you are doing! I am afraid they will kill you! Now you give right up,

Jok, and take a little whipping, and then go for your pass!"

Jok arose instantly, at the request of Mrs. C. As soon as the overseer was able to do so, he sprang up, rushed into the house, and seized a gun which he had loaded with shot the night previous. My informant, who was present, screamed out, "*he is going to shoot Jok!*" Mrs. C. caught hold of the gun, as he was leaving the house, exclaiming,

"You shan't kill Jok!"

"Yes I will shoot the nigger!"

"Remember my command, sir! Don't you kill that slave! You may *whip* him."

"May I whip him, madam, as much as I please?"

"You may whip him severely, but spare his life," replied Mrs. C., sternly.

"Do you give up, Jok?" said the overseer.

"Yes, master," was the submissive reply.

His coarse frock, which was all his clothing, was taken off; his thumbs tied together with a line; and the overseer, with a heavy green hide in his hand, led him out to the gin-house to flog him. Chloe went out around the stable, and came up behind the gin-house, where she could look in through the spaces between the logs, and see the punishment inflicted. The overseer was angry with the slave, and he whipped him with terrible severity, until, from suffering and loss of blood, he fainted and fell. Chloe ran to the house, and screamed,

"Mistress! I wish you would go out, for I believe the overseer has killed Jok!"

Mrs. C. hastened out, and finding him cut up shock,

ingly, she told the overseer to desist. She called some other slaves to convey Jok into the house, and then sent for a physician.

When the physician came, he said the slave could not live. He remained with him several hours, during which time he was constantly spitting blood, and uttering groans, as if in the agonies of death. Towards evening, however, his sufferings abated, and he finally recovered.

That mistress, and the overseer, and that slave boy and girl, were all *members of the same church.* And the overseer was superintendent of the Sabbath School connected with that church.

"He came into the house," said the lady who related the facts to me, "after whipping Jok, and washed his hands with as much composure as though nothing had occurred, and went off to church to take charge of the Sabbath School that Sabbath morning."

"Did the church discipline him for that act?" I inquired.

"This question was asked that mistress," said the teacher to me, "and she replied that the church could not do anything with the overseer, *as he had not violated the law.*"

"She was also asked, how she could commune with that overseer?"

'How can I refuse to do it," she replied, "unless the church censure him? And that I know they will not do!'"

XXII.

WAYSIDE NOTES.

"Rest, darlings, rest!
Never more with toil opprest
Shall we watch the western light
Slowly wane o'er fields of white.—
Daughter! upon limb of thine
Gilded chains shall never shine.
All thy mother's wrong and woe,
Dearest ones! ye ne'er shall know.
To my heart, exulting, pressed,
Rest, darlings, rest."

My note-book still contains a variety of incidents that can hardly be arranged into any particular class. The most of them I shall omit. But I have gathered up a few of them, that illustrate different phases of the slave system, and have thrown them together in this chapter.

THE SLAVE WIFE.

In the city of ——, there was a lumber merchant, who had several partners residing in Massachusetts. Mr. L.—for that was his name—went to a slave broker to hire a cook. It is not easy in the South to hire domestic help without hiring slaves. The broker informed Mr. L. that he had no slaves to let,— but that he had a fine quadroon girl that he would like to *sell*.

"I do not wish to buy, sir," replied Mr. L., "for my partners in Boston would not consent to purchase slaves."

"Well, I want you to look at her," said he. "She is a good girl, and will keep your boys straight at the mill; and I offer her so low that you had better buy than hire."

"Oh, I can't *buy* a slave; but I will look at her," said Mr. L., "if you desire it."

"*Nancy!*" said the broker, as he opened the door of a back room, into which no ray of light was admitted when the door was closed.

"When Nancy stepped into the room," said Mr. L., as he related the story to me, "I was never so shocked in my life; for I never saw a more beautiful female, apparently perfectly white, elegant, and, as I afterwards learned, highly accomplished.

"I wish you would buy me, sir," she exclaimed, with deep emotion;—for she saw at once that he would be a kind master. No one can read the countenance at a glance better than slaves. More than in the heavens, sunshine and storm are seen approaching in the glance of the master's eye. They study the human face as the sailors do the sky. No Northern man has failed to be surprised to see how his wants are often known by an intelligent slave before he has time to express them.

But Mr. L. had no idea of buying a slave. He hardly

knew why he had consented to look at this one. And when, in her beauty as well as sorrow, she stood before him, pleading for him to buy her, to save her from a worse fate, he hardly knew what to do. It is at this point that many a generous hearted man from the North has yielded, and become a slaveholder. But men who buy their first slave from motives of benevolence, perhaps with the intention of giving the boon of freedom at some future time, soon become familiarized to the system, — they forget the purpose to give their slaves their liberty, and finally they will buy and sell their fellowmen with as little compunction as those who have been educated under the influences of slavery. The only safe rule for any Northern man who may become a resident in the slave States is, never to buy a slave, under any circumstances, unless he can make the slave free at once. So thought Mr. L.; and therefore, as much as he pitied Nancy, and as indignant as he was that such a woman, in this Christian land, should be offered for sale, like the brutes, — he turned away, sorrowful, and left her to her fate.

The next day, — while Mr. L. was walking over one of the public malls, — Nancy, who had determined, if possible, to have an interview with him, and had obtained a pass for that purpose, ran up to him quickly, and exclaimed —

"I wish you would *buy* me, kind sir!"

"O don't say anything to me about that, *here!*" said Mr. L., thinking it was not safe for him to be seen talking with a slave, where so many were passing. But the second thought was that she was so white no one would suspect she was a slave, and he said to her —

"I pity you, Nancy, but I cannot buy you!"

"Will you stay, then, and listen to me?" implored the girl.

"A moment," replied Mr. L. "But say on, quickly."

"I was raised over here in South Carolina," said Nancy, pointing over the river. "My master was my father. It was always known in his family, and I lived as one of its members. He promised me, often, that he would give me free papers before he died. But he neglected to do it, and he was taken away suddenly. Two of his sons were dissipated, and the property had been so much diminished that they refused to give me my freedom. But they consented to let me have six years time, and if I could pay six hundred dollars to the administrator, then I should be free. I worked four years, at various kinds of sewing, and during that time I paid four hundred dollars. I was acquainted with a young slaveholder who was brought up in the same neighborhood where I was, in whom I had great confidence. He came forward and proposed to pay the other two hundred dollars, and make me his wife. I accepted the offer. He went to the administrator, paid over the money, and took a deed of me in his own name. I did not inquire how the matter was adjusted, as I had no suspicion that any future trouble would arise from it.

"After we had lived together several years, and I had become the mother of two beautiful daughters — now five and six years of age — a family quarrel arose between us, for which no virtuous wife and mother could blame *me;* and, as the result, my cruel husband has sent me here *to be sold.* Oh! can you not save me and my little children from such a fate?"

Mr. L. made further inquiries, and found that her story was true. Her happiness was but a dream, and it had vanished. Her home was desolate. Under that inexorable law of slavery—*partus sequiter ventrem*—her darling daughters, like herself, were liable to all the terrible contingencies of the slave's lot. And as human affection, and plighted faith, had failed to save her, so it might be with them. For them, as well as for herself, was she in agony and despair.

I will not prolong the story, except to say that by the noble efforts of Mr. L. this family were rescued from a fate worse than death. I met her afterwards in the cars, on her way to a city in the interior, to reside in the family of a clergyman. She had received her free papers, and the cup of her joy was full. A shade of sorrow would occasionally flit across her countenance,—for ties sacred to her had been severed,—but in the greatness of her deliverance she forgot all things besides. It was meet that such a flood of joy should sweep away, for a time, at least, all the traces of her sorrow. How many like her are there still in bondage, upon whose cheerless, weary lives no ray of hope has ever shone! He, only, who knoweth all things, can tell!

READING UNCLE TOM'S CABIN.

I had the pleasure of hearing Uncle Tom's Cabin read to a company in one of the planting districts. It was reported in the place that a man was coming to fiinish reading that "*wonderful novel*" to all — "except slaves" — who would assemble at K. N.'s long mule stable on a certain night. After the crowd had gathered, and the reading had commenced, I entered the room silently, to witness the scene. The reader was seated on a stack of corn in the middle of the long, narrow stable, reading by a small oil lamp. There was no other light in the room, and I felt very happy to enjoy the privilege of a seat on the sill, in a corner so dark that I was not seen. I counted nearly sixty heads between me and the light. How many there were on the other side, I could not see. But the noisy cheers gave me the impression that the ship was well balanced. I remained until one o'clock in the morning, and then left before any others came away. I had previously read the book, and therefore concluded to retire and sleep a little; but I was subsequently informed that no others left until the volume was finished.

The reader was frequently interrupted by remarks from his auditors, who took the liberty, as he went along, to compare the characters described in the book with their own acquaintances. There was a slaveholder in the place by the name of Yopp, who owned a slave girl called Nancy. It seemed that Nancy answered most accurately the description of Topsy; for when the reading had fully developed Topsy's peculiar characteristics, a slaveholder's wife cried out,

"Now wasn't that girl just like old Yopp's Nancy?"

And they had their St. Clares, and Legrees, and all

the other persons and things of which the "Cabin" was constructed. There was no intimation from any one present that the picture was overwrought.

While I was at Athens, Georgia, I learned that several boxes of the "Cabin" were destroyed in that city, while on their way to Alabama. But the merchant who ordered them, whom I afterwards met, told me that all the masters gained by that bonfire, was the sale of as many more; for he was determined that his family and his neighbors should read it.

"If there was not a syllable of truth in it," said he, "still I would have it read, as it is the *best novel* that was ever written!"

SLAVERY AND CASTE.

While I was spending a few days at G., where several young men were employed in hewing timber, one of them cut his foot badly. I sewed up and dressed the wound, and gave him a pair of stockings and a pair of rubbers, as he had none of his own. His name was William Hardison. He expressed much gratitude for my kindness, and afterwards he gave me a full history of his family. He was a steady, industrious, intelligent young man.

"My father," said he, "was a Northern man. My mother was a native of this State, and owned slaves when my father married her. Once we were wealthy, and our family moved in the best circles. But my father became dissipated, wasted all the property, and sold all the slaves except one, an old man, who ran away. Two hounds followed him. One of them was an old dog, that had caught a great many negroes; but the slave killed him with a club. The other dog forced him into a tree.

"When my father came up, and found the slave had killed his favorite dog, he ordered him to come down from the tree. After he had come down, he pointed his rifle towards the slave, and commanded him to cut up a hind quarter of the old dog, and eat it raw, with the hide and hair. Pompey was forced to obey, but he died before the next morning. By this fatal calamity, our family were cut loose from the society of slaveholders, with whom we had always associated on terms of equality. My miserable father died soon after, and left us in a truly deplorable condition, without food, without friends! I went to a slaveholder one day, — a neighbor who was always kind and obliging, *while we were slaveholders,* — and informed him that we had nothing to eat; and I asked him if he would give my mother and the children some bread.

'No,' said he, 'I don't want you around here, troubling me; I have niggers enough to eat my corn.'

"I then asked, with great importunity, if he would permit me to go to the corn crib, and take home a few ears of corn to boil for supper. This favor also was denied me. This family always exchanged visits with us in our prosperous days, and nothing ever occurred to create the least disaffection, or occasion the slightest neglect, until we lost caste by becoming poor and losing our slaves."

"Instead of showing favor to non-slaveholding whites,"

said Mr. H., "the slaveholders oppress them in every possible manner, without regard to their legal rights. If they want to drive a poor man out of the neighborhood, they will buy the land on which his shanty sets, and then burn it. Sometimes, poor people build log houses on lands of which no owner can be found at the time, and thus these houses are left at the mercy of whoever may subsequently obtain possession of the lands."

"Is there no law in this State against such things, Mr. H.? And will not public opinion prevent a man from burning his neighbor's house?" I inquired.

"I know not what the law is," answered Mr. H.; "but I know that slaveholders do as they please with the property of nonslaveholders, who have, in any way, displeased them. And I state the fact, as within my own knowledge, that the poor are sometimes compelled to leave a neighborhood after their dwellings have thus been destroyed by fire. And often, even when the poor man has a good claim to the land on which his house stands, a slaveholder will set up a false claim to it, and drive him away. The fact is so generally understood that the courts favor the slaveholders, and there is so little hope of obtaining redress by law, that the nonslaveholders usually submit rather than contend with them."

The degradation of women is a mark of heathenism the world over. It is one of the boasted triumphs of Christianity — justly so — that it has always tended to elevate and improve the condition of women. And though there is a kind of refinement and elegance among the females of slaveholding families, — the tendency of the system is to degrade them. Especially is this the case among the slaves, and the nonslaveholders.

Of the former I hardly need to speak. The female slaves cannot be otherwise than degraded. Subjected at all times to the passions of the whites, chastity and refinement are out of the question. They are stripped entirely naked to be punished, not only on the plantations, but by the city marshals in the cities, to whom the masters send them for this purpose. And often they are exposed in public for sale, in the same condition. Let the Northern tourist visit the slave market, or the whipping post, and he will frequently behold scenes at which the most degraded African, just imported, would hang his head in shame! A slave woman, entirely naked, surrounded by a profane and vulgar crowd, while she writhes under the lash, or is offered, for purposes of prostitution, to the highest bidder! Such is the "Christianizing influence" of which the advocates of the slave trade so loudly boast!

Nor do the slave women suffer alone in this respect. Among the poor, ignorant, degraded, intemperate nonslaveholders, the condition of the females is wretched beyond description. Especially is this the case in those families that have been owners of slaves. The father and the sons are either so dissipated that they make no provision for their families, or they are already in drunkards' graves. Often have I seen women who have been brought up in luxury, all unused to labor, thus compelled by reverse of fortune to work in the field. Their former acquaintances, among slaveholders, neither know nor care any thing about their condition.

In Wilkinson county, Ga., I saw two young ladies at work in the field. They told me that the year before, 1852, they performed all the labor, — plowing, planting, hoeing, &c., and raised three bales of cotton. They lived in Emmet, near the Central railroad. This cotton was worth there about forty dollars a bale. They had a widowed mother, and this was their only means of support.

In another county on the Oconee river I saw an aged grand-mother, a daughter, and three grand-daughters, all at work in the same field, hoeing cotton. They had been slaveholders; but the father of the three youngest had squandered his property in dissipation, and dying in poverty, the family were compelled to labor in this way to keep themselves from starvation. Such instances are common throughout the whole South.

PREJUDICE AGAINST COLOR.

The anti-slavery cause has encountered no greater obstacle in the free States, than prejudice against color. As absurd and wicked as it is, it has been almost universal, — excluding the colored race not only from social position, but from churches and schools, — from hotels, steamboats, and railroad cars. This unchristian prejudice is wearing away, — and yet, during the present year, one of the most accomplished ladies in the country has often been put to serious inconvenience, even in New England, by certain brainless puppets of fashion, who affected to look down upon her with contempt, — unconscious that they thus exposed *themselves* to the contempt of all those whose good opinion is of any consequence.

This prejudice against color has not only had a tendency to check all sympathy for the slaves, — but it has been the source of many foolish objections to emancipation. Men and women who carry on their bodies the unwashed filth of years — covered, perhaps, with purple and fine linen — turn up their noses with horror at the idea of having a "nigger" around them. And at the thought of emancipation they picture to themselves an innumerable company of slaves, "turned loose" to overrun the North, as terrible as the locusts of Egypt!

It is somewhat surprising to a Northern man to find none of this prejudice in the South. If the slaves could be set at liberty to-day, there would be nothing of this kind to exclude them from genteel society. The whites are accustomed now to associate with them as intimately, though not on the same terms of equality, as with each other. You find none of that exquisite, rose-water sensitiveness in the South which some men, and I am sorry to say, some *women*, even, in the free States, are so fond of exhibiting. If a colored man owns slaves, — and I regret to say that there are a few such in the South, — he is treated as courteously, and with as much respect, wherever he travels, as any thin skinned white dandy who may chance to be in his company. I have always regarded the Northern apologist for slavery as infinitely more worthy of condemnation than the slaveholder himself, trained up from his youth with Southern views and feelings. So this prejudice against color is a type of meanness beyond anything which the South can produce. The Southron would scorn it, in any such sense as it prevails in the free States.

We had in our company of passengers, on the way from Georgia to Pennsylvania, a middle aged slaveholder, with a black woman and her infant child. This gentleman uniformly occupied the same seat in the cars with the colored lady, whom he treated with constant attention. He conversed with her freely and politely, — dandled her baby on his knee, and for ought that I knew, was her husband. Nor did I hear any intimation, from any one in the company, that it was in the least degree improper or offensive to have a colored person in the car or coach, until we reached Philadelphia.

Soon after the train left that city for the North, a great stir was made in the car in which I was seated, because a colored gentleman had taken a seat there. This gentleman was a Mr. Moore, formerly a slave. He had resided a few years in Philadelphia, where he had married an intelligent colored lady, and had accumulated a property worth some two thousand dollars. The fugitive slave bill had passed, and his master had come to that city to arrest him. He had only time to fly, after notice of his danger, without taking any measures to secure his property. He was a fine looking, gentlemanly man; and when he came into the cars, he was neatly dressed.

I was sitting on the front seat, facing the passengers, when the conductor went to Mr. Moore, and informed him that the passengers objected to his occupying a seat in that car, and that he must therefore take a seat in one of another class. Mr. M. followed the conductor forward to the door. I rose up, and said to the conductor that I had just traveled hundreds of miles in the slave States, — that I had heard no one complain because colored persons were allowed to sit in the same cars with us, — and that I felt indignant and ashamed to see a distinction made as soon as we came into a free State. And I told him that if any individual must leave that car on that account, I would give up my seat to the colored passenger, and leave, myself. Dr. Bailey, of the National Era, who was sitting near, also interceded; and Mr. Moore was allowed to remain. How long will the people of the North cherish a feeling so repugnant to all the dictates not only of humanity, but of common sense?

XXIII.

THE GIANT SLAVE.

"But slaves who once conceive the glowing thought
Of freedom, in that hope itself possess
All that the contest calls for — spirit, strength,
The scorn of danger, the undying hope,
The surest presage of the good they seek."

COWPER.

MUCH has been said of the equality of races. The discussion generally is profitless. Races, like individuals, are unlike; and therefore the question of equality can never be settled. Each, in some qualities, excels the others. With all the boasting of our Anglo-Saxon stock, it is undeniable that the African race, under equal advantages, would excel us in music and poetry. And who shall say that the fine arts are not quite as important as the more solid endowments which, perhaps, the Creator has given in greater measure to us? The rights of man are dependent on neither. *These* God has given alike to all, of every nation, of every degree of culture.

It is a curious fact that, even among barbarous tribes of men, we find occasionally one whom the All-wise has rarely endowed, — one who possesses powers and abilities far above his fellows. Such was Black Hawk among the Indians. And in the South there may be found here and there a slave of remarkable strength, both of body and mind. They appear to be exceptions to the general rule, standing forth among their oppressed and degraded brethren,

> "above the rest
> In shape and gesture proudly emminent."

Such, undoubtedly, was "Dread," whose terrible death I have already recorded. It was not my fortune to see him, — as he fell a sacrifice to the slave system before I visited the neighborhood where he lived, and suffered, and died. But I gathered up what little could be learned of his history, and leave it in this volume, a feeble tribute to his memory.

"The best temperance lecturer I ever heard," said a Southern merchant to me, "was a giant negro up river, whom I once heard speak on that subject." This was "Hannibal," the subject of this sketch.

I had occasion to cross the —— river. It was a dark, stormy day, and the waters were swollen by the freshet. The river was deep, and wide, and the ferry boat was drawn across by means of a rope, fastened to a tree on either side. I noticed, as I entered the boat, that the ferryman — a slave — was a man of giant stature, and prodigious muscular development. He was about six and a half feet high, of admirable proportions, and though not by any means corpulent, he weighed, as I afterwards learned, over three hundred pounds. Though the current was strong, he held the boat steady by the rope, and rapidly drew it across the river. Like all slaves who mingle in good society, he was affable and polite in his manners; but unlike most slaves, instead of that cringing look which nothing but a consciousness of degradation can produce, there was a native dignity and manliness in his bearing, which even his condition could not conceal; — a divinity that not even slavery could tarnish or degrade. As he assisted me to the shore, he asked,

"Are you not from the North, sir?"

"Why do you think so?" I asked, with some surprise.

"O," said he, "I have been across the river with so many persons, not only from all parts of this country, but from foreign countries, that I can generally tell where any one is from."

"Well," said I, "you have guessed right in my case. I am from the North."

I then left the ferryman alone, and walked to the village, half a mile distant. During the night, a large cypress tree, which the waters had brought down from its native bank, was carried against Hannibal's ferry rope, uprooting the trees to which it was fastened on either side. The next morning I came down to the river, intending to recross. The fact was known in the village that the rope had been carried away, and that no one could cross until the waters had abated so that another guide rope could be stretched over. Hence no one, — except myself, who had not heard that the rope was gone, — came down to the ferry house. This was a little log hut, of which Hannibal was the only occupant; although he had had a wife and two children, nine miles above, on the river, until within a few weeks. As I stepped into his lowly cabin, which had neither window nor door, Hannibal arose, and repeating my name, he addressed me freely and cordially, as if I had been an old school mate. He said that he desired me to excuse this familiarity, as he had been up to the tavern, and had learned my name; and he earnestly requested me to inform him how the free colored people were getting along in my State.

I saw, at a glance, that I was in the presence of no ordinary man. He had a broad, high forehead, a very large head, containing a massive brain, active and powerful; and, although apparently sincere and friendly, yet he looked so metaphysical, dark, and mysterious withal, that I feared to express any sympathy for him or for his race, lest he should betray me to his master.

"I know but little about the colored people," I replied. "I never saw a negro in the town where I was brought up; and I advise a slave who has a kind master to be contented where he is."

Hannibal looked sad and dejected at my reply, but I was afraid to trust him. I left him abruptly, and strolled up the river a mile or two, looking at the magnificent forests of oak and pine that covered the banks. A few hours passed, and I came back again. When I walked softly and slowly up to Hannibal's hut, and looked in upon him, I just had a glimpse of a small, dingy book, as it was flung from his hand under a board, by the side of the rock chimney.

"Hannibal! can you read?" said I.

He sat motionless so long before speaking, that I began to fear I had either troubled him, or that he was intending to trouble me, when he sprang up from his stool, looked me firmly in the face, and asked, earnestly,

"Wont you betray me, master?"

"Betray you? Hannibal! No; I am your friend."

"My friend?" said he, with deep emotion. "What am I to understand by that?"

"Why, that I am not only *your* friend, but the friend of your *race*," said I.

"Indeed, sir!" ejaculated the slave. "And in what way are you the friend of my race?"

I now saw plainly that he wanted a friend, and I replied, "I wish that you all enjoyed the same liberty that I enjoy."

He turned to the chimney, raised the board, and took out the book. It was Robinson Crusoe! This was the first time he had read it; and he was so deeply absorbed in the story,—not expecting any one down from the village to cross the river,—that I had surprised him.

"*There*," said he, handing me the book with a trembling hand, "is what I was reading. Did you ever read that book, master?"

"Oh, yes, Hannibal! That was one of the first books I ever read when I was a little boy. It is a beautiful story, too."

"A *story*, master! I thought it was *real*. I am sorry it was made up; for I was thinking how happy I should be on such an island, where I could be *master* awhile."

"But how came you to be able to read it, Hannibal?"

He went to the hiding place, and took out Garrison's work on colonization, two copies of Leavitt's Emancipator, and a mutilated copy of the New Testament, saying,

"I have begged these of Northern men,—promising them that after they were gone, I would drop them where the slaveholders would find them. Now, master, I will tell you; only one man in the world, besides you, has ever known that I can read a word. That was my young master John. My mother nursed him at the same time she nursed me. We were just about the same age. When master John was sent to the academy here, and learned his letters, he taught them to me. As soon as my old master found out that John was teaching me, he forbade it. But I loved John, and he loved me also. I always had considerable influence over him, and could persuade or hire him to do anything for me. I told him that I would never reveal the fact, if he would teach me all that he learned himself. John had confidence in me, and whatever he was taught at school, he taught me. When he began to read Latin, he called me *master;* for he left his grammar with me nights, and I learned faster than he did by day. Sometimes he came to our hut Sundays, and he said I gave him better instruction than he got at the academy.

"And now, master, I will tell you why I asked you about the free colored people at the North. My young master used to tell me that he meant to make me free; but he died suddenly, and nothing was done about it. My old master has always been kind to me, and I have always tried to be contented with my fate, although my labors have been very hard, and my comforts few. *I had a wife, but she was taken from me two weeks ago!* She belonged to another man, nine miles above here. I never let her know that I could read; for I knew that she was liable at any time to be sold, and in many ways the fact would become known. She had a cruel master, and did not have enough corn to eat. I used to carry food and other things to her and to my two little boys. My master knew it, and did not forbid it. I complained of the treatment which my wife received from her master; for I loved Nelly, and always shall! Her master hated me, after he found out that I talked about his being a hard master to my wife; and to punish me, he sold her to be carried off two hundred miles up river. My master offered seven hundred dollars more for Nelly than she was sold for; but her master would not have me gratified so much as to have her live with me. Another man,—whose wife lives in this place,—was sold by Nelly's master at the same time, and taken to the same plantation where she is. He ran away and came back here to see his wife, and he told me that Nelly wanted him to let me know where she was.

"Now," he continued, "I am resolved to run away. I have three hundred dollars by me that my master has no knowledge of; and I shall either go up to the neighborhood where Nelly is, find a hiding place in the woods, get her with me, hire the slaves to bring us provisions, and so live together as long as we can, and suffer whatever may come upon us;—or I will make the attempt to reach the North, where I can be free. I am now forty years old. I have often cursed God for my fate! Death, to me, would always have been a welcome relief! I prefer it *now* to the prospect of living longer in my present condition. And while I have the strength, and the *will*, I am resolved on *one* effort for a change, come what may! Can I get to a free State?"

"How?" said I. "Across the country?"

"O, no!" he replied, quickly. "It is a long way; and I am so much larger than most slaves, every one who sees me would demand a pass. All the hounds, and half the devils who own them, would chase me. I should probably be taken, or *killed*, in a short time; *both if either, I tell you!* But can't I go down river in a light *bateau*, in the night, and find some friend in the city, who will help me on board a vessel bound North, and so escape?"

"Oh, no!" said I. "There would not be one chance in a thousand for you to reach a free State in that way. But I can plan to make you free in a single day, after I arrive at New York."

"How? How?" he asked, with great earnestness.

"I can raise the money," I replied, "to purchase your freedom."

"Ah, sir!" said the despairing slave, "the man would be shot, who should come here, with any sum of money, proposing to buy me *and carry me North*. The slaveholders here know that I know all about slavery, and that I could tell what I know; and never shall I be allowed to go to a free State with their consent."

"I used to talk on the subject of temperance. The slaves were very intemperate here, and my master told me that I might hold meetings, and talk to them. Soon after I commenced talking publicly, the slaves began to quit drinking. They came a great distance to hear me. Not only the slaves, but their masters also came in crowds. The latter expressed great astonishment that I could use so good language, and they said it must be *inspiration,* — not knowing that I went to the academy with John, and that he taught me much of what little he learned at college, after he came home from the North."

I suggested several plans for his escape, but no one that was feasible, in his opinion. I asked him if it was a common thing in that neighborhood, where there were five hundred slaves, for them to separate husband and wife. He said,

"I and Scipio, my half brother, whose wife has just been sold, were reckoning up last night, how many we know who have been separated since we were married, six years ago; and we reckoned up thirty!"

I remained there several days, and during that time had several interviews with this remarkable slave. And the more I saw him, the more strongly was I impressed with his natural greatness and power, — not, indeed, entirely destitute of cultivation. What would I not have given to deliver him from the terrible load that pressed him down! We often conversed on the subject of his escape, and I left him, not without some hope of soon meeting him in a land where "the slave would be a man."

About the time I was ready to start, the waters of the

river had partially subsided, and Hannibal's master, with Scipio, came down to stretch across another rope. I concluded to take the same boat with them. The current was still strong, as the river had not yet settled within its banks; and it was therefore necessary to row up stream farther than usual before crossing, or the current would carry us down below the landing on the opposite shore. Below this landing there was an alder swamp, through which we must wade if we fell below the wharf. Before we had gone up far enough to insure a safe landing, the master ordered the boat to be headed across. Hannibal remonstrated, and said that we should certainly fall below the wharf. But the master said, — "head her about," — not regarding the opinion of the slave, who had a life-long acquaintance with the river.

He soon perceived, however, that the current was stronger than he had anticipated, and that we were in danger of being carried below the wharf; and he said to Hannibal, "you don't pull, boy." The next dip, the oar fell deep in the waters, and the "boy" pulled so hard that he shivered it in pieces! It was made of sound hard pine, and was about four inches in diameter. I expected to hear the master scold when he heard the crash of the oar, and saw that we should fail to reach the wharf; but he laughed, and exclaimed,

"It is a gone case with us now, boys! We have got to wade."

And so it was. Instead of being landed at the wharf, we were run into the swamp below. The master jumped out where the cold water — for it was winter — was up to his waist. But the boys said the passenger was not to blame, and they pulled the boat over and through the alders, about forty rods, where I stepped out in water so shallow as not to run over my boots.

Here I left *Hannibal* — receiving in sadness his parting blessing. And his last words to me were, — "*I shall start within a fortnight.*"

XXIV.

THE ETHIOPIAN SOCRATES.

"Yes, dark-souled chieftain! — if the light
  Of mild Religion's heavenly ray
Unveiled not to thy mental sight
  The lowlier and the purer way, —
Let not the favored white man name
Thy stern appeal, with words of blame."

WHITTIER.

FEW Northern men, probably, have ever had a better view of slavery than I had. It may seem to those who have read the preceding pages that I have portrayed only its darker features. To some extent this is true. An *inside view of slavery* could not be otherwise. Whatever fairer and better aspects it presents, they are all external, and have so often been presented to the public that it has been no part of my purpose to reproduce them. And while I do not deny the truth of such representations, as exhibiting simply the *outside* of the system, I claim for that which is less exposed, and less noticed, at least an equal importance, in order fully to understand the subject.

I cannot bring this volume to a close more appropriately than with the following story, from a recent number of the *N. Y. Independent.* It is from the pen of that beautiful and popular writer, who, I believe, is only known to the public by her *nomme de plume,* "Minnie Myrtle." She assures me that the narrative may be relied upon as correct in every particular, even in the language used by the poor slave. It was related to her by a citizen of Baltimore, a distinguished member of the Society of Friends, who received it from the Judge who presided at the trial. No one can read it without feeling that there are powers and capacities, both of doing and suffering, in the African race, far above what he has been accustomed to believe. And if, in view of such facts, there are any who are willing to volunteer with their apologies for slaveholders, to debauch the public heart with "South-Side Views," and Scriptural defenses, I am fully pursuaded that the only way such men could be convinced of the enormities of slavery would be to apply the iron to their own limbs, and the lash to their own backs, until they could "remember those in bonds *as bound with them.*"

Many years ago, said an aged gentleman to me, I was traveling among the monntains of Virginia, when one of those terrible storms arose which are known only among the mountains; when the rain falls in sheets, and the thunder roars in one continuous crash and peal, seeming as if the hills would be shaken from their foundations, and the heavens gleam like a mass of fire which the drenching waters cannot quench. We were a long distance from any village, and for a long time looked in vain for a temporary shelter, but at length came in sight of a small inn, which our little party filled to overflowing. Soon another party arrived, which the pitiless storm had driven to the same shelter. But the landlord was more pitiless still, and rudely told them that he had no room for more. But as we were all of one family, we offered to share with our new comers half our own accommodations, and were soon on such terms of acquaintanceship with a cultivated gentleman and his intelligent daughters, as a storm and the close proximity of a country inn know best how to produce.

Before dark the storm had ceased, and the moon arose in all her queenly beauty, inviting us to sit upon the broad piazza and enjoy the evening air. Our new friends were from a more southern clime, and commenced conversation by asking if we had heard of a sad instance of wrong and crime which occurred not long ago in a neighboring county. As things of that kind did not then so frequently find their way into the public prints as in these days, we had seen no allusion to the matter, and listened with unspeakable emotion whilst the gentleman related to us the following story:

"A Southern trader had been commissioned to purchase a blacksmith, and to pay any price for one of superior skill and qualifications, wherever he might be found. In his roamings about the country he heard of one belonging to a rich lady, but doubted about being able to obtain him, as necessity would not compel her to part with him, and he had been long a faithful servant in her family. She was sick, too, and would not, as a dying act, wish to sell from his wife and children one who had proved of such invaluable service to her.

"But a thousand dollars proved a temptation which even a dying woman could not resist, and the bargain was finished, and the soul and body of a noble man consigned as property to a heartless trader, without a word of consultation with him on the subject. On being called and informed of the transfer, he exclaimed in bitter agony, 'What have I done to deserve this? Have I not been a faithful servant, laboring night and day for my mistress, without ever in a single instance refusing to obey her orders?' Here his voice choked so that he could not speak, as he seemed overwhelmed with a sense of the wrong which had been done him, and of his helplessness; but he soon added, 'Well, I know I am a poor slave, and must submit to my fate, but it is hard.'

"The trader was neither moved to compassion nor kindness, and he approached to place upon his limbs the galling fetters, which were only the symbols of a more galling servitude, when the negro ventured again to remonstrate. He did not ask for freedom, or to be returned to his mistress. Alas! the thought of her must have been bitterness indeed to him now — but he asked the one little boon of being permitted to see his wife and children before he was separated from them forever.

"'I know,' he said, 'I am your slave. You have bought me and paid for me, and I am bound to obey you This I will not refuse to do. But I have a wife and little children two miles from here, with whom I have lived very happy. Will you not permit me to see them once more before I go? I promise solemnly I will return to-morrow morning, and go with you and do your bidding without a murmur.'

"'No,' said the trader, 'you cannot go.'

"'But oh, it is very hard that I cannot see my wife and children before I go, and bid them farewell. I am a man of truth, and I promise faithfully to return to-morrow morning if you will let me go.'

"'No,' was the indignant answer; 'you cannot go; and you may as well come along without any more fuss.'

"'Well,' answered the honest and injured husband and father, 'I must submit. I cannot help myself. But I tell you plainly I will never serve you; I will never perform a single act for your benefit.'

"'Oh, I am not troubled about that,' said the trader; 'I know how to deal with such as you, and have no fears about your obeying my commands.' And he placed the manacles upon his wrists and ankles, gave him a blow from his whip, and he was driven away.

"How the proud spirit chafed and writhed in the fetters! But, as he said, there was no help. For several days he was detained at a station-house, till a large gang was collected, when they were marched off towards their Southern destination. There was no further remonstrance, and no attempt at escape; till with feet sore and bleeding from days and nights of constant tramping upon thorny paths and burning sands, they encamped upon the borders of a running stream for a little rest.

The men reclined in their chains upon the ground, and the women were strewed in heaps among the baggage of the wagons. The moon shone clear and bright, and scarcely a breath of air stirred the leaves of the trees above their heads, and all were asleep. It was not a night to favor crime; yet revenge burned so hotly in the bosom of the outraged negro that he could not longer delay. His trade had made him familiar with iron links, and with a little application of his skill his bonds were loosened, and he was free. But he did not attempt to fly. He crept stealthily to the tent of the trader, and with one blow of the axe severed his head from his body!—then returned to his resting place and slept soundly till morning!

"The break of day revealed the terrible deed, and the excitement soon spread from the negro camp to the neighboring settlements, and crowds gathered in eager curiosity to learn the particulars of the crime. Several were put to the torture in attempts to make them confess, but the guilty one not wishing others to suffer for what he had done, came forward and gave himself up to justice. Double manacles were put upon his limbs, and he was confined in jail until the day of trial. On being told by the judge that he would have the benefit of counsel and every advantage which the law could give, notwithstanding his confession, he again disclaimed all pretensions to innocence, and expressed no desire to live. 'I killed the man,' said he, 'and I did it after deliberate reflection, and still think his hard-hearted cruelty justified the act. I am not sorry.'

"There was a sort of mock trial, at the end of which the verdict of 'Guilty,' was solemnly rendered, and the accused was asked if he had anything to say to the court. With great dignity, and no visible emotion he arose and said:

"'I am grateful for your kindness, and for the opportunity you gave me of escaping death; but I have no wish to live. I am cruelly separated from all that is most dear to me, and life is no longer of any value. I do not wish to live, and I am not afraid to die, and I have only one favor to ask of earthly friends. I would like to know that the day of my execution is fixed on the 4th of July, which will soon be here. It is the day you celebrate as the anniversary of your emancipation from the slavery of a foreign despotism. If you grant me this request, the day will be the anniversary of my emancipation from a bondage much more galling than was ever inflicted upon you. From that day I shall be as free as you!'

"He who spoke was of Ethiop blackness, but his manner was as calm as that of the Athenian philosopher when the hemlock was presented to his lips, and his whole demeanor as dignified and respectful. Among the audience there was a breathless stillness, which for a long time was not interrupted, and all departed under the influence of deep and impressive solemnity.

"Neither in the prison nor on the scaffold was there any change in the guilty man, and nothing could wring from him anything like a confession that he had sinned in taking the life of one so inhuman. He had rid the earth of a monster, and was willing to die for the deed.

"His mind was in the darkness of heathenism, and we leave him for God to judge. And we also leave Him to judge those who keep in darkness millions of immortal souls, and so imbrutalize and degrade them that conscience is without life, and deliberate crime without horror.

"But it is pleasant to add that there were accounts immediately of the liberation of many who had been kept in bondage in that region, proving that the dying words of a negro could affect the heart."

"Oh, where's the man so lowly,
Condemned to things unholy,
Who, could he burst
His chains at first,
Would pine beneath them slowly?

What soul whose wrongs degrade it,
Would wait till time decayed it,
When thus its wing
At once may spring
To the throne of Him who made it?"

www.ingramcontent.com/pod-product-compliance
Lightning Source LLC
LaVergne TN
LVHW020228110826
845151LV00003B/861

* 9 7 8 1 4 2 5 5 3 1 3 3 1 *